COLLECTING  ART NOUVEAU

Philippe Garner

TREASURE PRESS

FOREWORD

There is a certain paradox in writing a book which aims to
discuss Art Nouveau, and which is also a book for collectors.

Although the Art Nouveau style flourished a mere three-
quarters of a century ago, good examples of the style are
already considered as museum material. Very high prices have
been paid for the finest and rarest examples of the style, and
the choicest objects are out of the reach of most collectors.
There is much low-quality Art Nouveau available on the
market. Rather than highlight the mediocre, however, simply
because it is more readily available, my aim has been to
demonstrate just how good turn-of-the-century design and
craftsmanship could be. This book, therefore, presents an
ideal collection, encompassing objects outstanding for both
design and execution. Any collector trained to appreciate this
quality, and with such a high standard always in mind, will
be able to select his own objects with great discrimination.
This collector will also derive pleasure from handling a mobile
collection of objects the standard of which he is always
endeavouring to increase. All great collectors are ruthless and
follow the principle that the art of collecting is more a process
of eliminating than of amassing objects.   P.G.

(*title page illustration*) A decorative cast iron cross designed by
Hector Guimard for the graves of the French soldiers who died in
the First World War

First published in Great Britain in 1974 by
The Hamlyn Publishing Group Limited under the title Art Nouveau for
Collectors.
This edition published in 1989 by
Treasure Press
81 Fulham Road
Michelin House
London SW3 6RB

Copyright © the Hamlyn Publishing Group Limited 1974

ISBN 1 85051 449 6

PRODUCED BY MANDARIN OFFSET
PRINTED AND BOUND IN SINGAPORE

CONTENTS

INTRODUCTION

Art Nouveau was a radical movement within the decorative arts, developing internationally, and lasting at its full strength over a period of about ten years from 1895 to 1905, though it lingered on in certain instances till around 1910. Too many books on Art Nouveau have started by listing the many alternative names that have been attached to this manifestation. This list, with the various and sometimes contradictory nuances implicit in the different names, only adds to an initial feeling of confusion. For the term 'Art Nouveau' in itself seems paradoxical to many. It is not easy, at first glance, to understand how the same stylistic title can be applied at once to objects constructed entirely of tightly controlled straight lines, such as we find in Scottish or Austrian Art Nouveau, and to objects conceived as the most elaborate series of convolutions such as we encounter especially in French Art Nouveau.

Art Nouveau was, in fact, a series of styles, having in common the desire to be 'new', to break away from the non-constructive historicising tendencies prevalent during the nineteenth century and seeking an aesthetic in keeping with the demands of the new age of technology that was fast over-taking traditional modes of design and manufacture. Whilst these were the essential aims, few designers fully succeeded in achieving them. Although 'novelty' was the ideal, it is possible to trace precursors of the style, and its evolution, through the last third of the nineteenth century. It is also possible to trace elements clearly borrowed from other styles, or absorbed from other cultures; thus we find motifs that are revivals of the Celtic, of the Baroque, or the Rococco, or borrowed from Japan. Few designers could be said to have achieved a full, unshackled 'modern' style.

The desire for fantasy and invention was too strong, and in many instances Art Nouveau, almost in spite of itself, became the last great decadent style, the final flowering of a romantic exoticism. Such extreme versions of Art Nouveau were delightful, but short-lived. Around the mid 1890s the presence was making itself felt, in its full force, of a style which craved

Occasional table with fruitwood marquetry. Emile Gallé, about 1900

novelty and loathed traditionalism. The energy of this new movement was soon spent, however, in self-indulgent extravagances and elaborations.

By 1910 this high Art Nouveau style was dead, having paid the price for its too-neurotic exuberance. While certain designers, especially the French, explored the decadent 'hot house' possibilities of the style as an anaesthetic for their fears of the Machine Age, other schools of Art Nouveau defeated their own aims and exposed their essential insecurity by seeking their escape not in a truly forward-looking ideal of modernism, but in the dead-end romanticism of a return to the glorious Medieval age of craft. Closely allied with this emphasis on the justification of craft is the important aspect of Art Nouveau theory which worked towards destroying the arbitrary barriers between the 'fine' and the 'applied' arts. Art Nouveau theorists decried as meaningless the traditionally held belief that art could only manifest itself through painting, drawing or sculpture. At last it was realised that the design of the most everyday object, bell push, teapot, chair, or light fitting, demanded as great an appreciation of form and proportion as did the creation of a non-functional three-dimensional object. As a part of this synthesis of the arts one finds, for instance, the furniture of Hector Guimard discussed as sculpture, and one sees Toulouse-Lautrec distilling all his artistry in the design of theatre posters. This attempt at synthesis also explains the versatility of so many designers around the turn of the century.

Commentators on the Art Nouveau movement tend to agree that, although the British version of the style was seldom as adventurous as that of other countries, it was in Britain that the greatest momentum was built up during the nineteenth century in preparing the path for this style. Certain critics have pinpointed William Blake's drawings as the very first anticipatory signals. The two key names in the evolution of Art Nouveau theory in Britain, however, are those of John Ruskin and of William Morris. Ruskin, an art critic whose writings span the years between 1843 and 1889, proposed simple yet exacting principles of design. He believed that

Chair designed by Arthur Heygate Mackmurdo, 1881

The Pilgrim and the Rose, a tapestry designed by Burne-Jones, 1901

beauty could only be the inevitable product of healthy and ennobling labour; an object should above all be fit for its purpose and, in seeking this fitness, the designer should neither imitate nor derive ideas from former styles: let nature in her logic be his source of inspiration. Ruskin despised the pursuit of an arbitrarily sophisticated 'perfection' of finish, in which the signs of labour, the irregularities of hand labour, were effaced. He idealised the creative craftsman in a socialistic doctrine that abolished the stigma associated with manual labour. Ruskin pushed his ideas relentlessly and his fervour captivated many designers who endeavoured to put his theories into practice. The greatest disciple of Ruskin, and himself an important social theorist, was William Morris. Whilst proving himself a gifted designer and creating a style of decoration that was the prelude to Art Nouveau, Morris's work serves only to demonstrate the loopholes and inconsistencies in Ruskin's and his own theories. Both men cherished a notion of 'honesty'. For Morris, this involved a need on the part of the artist/craftsman to be true to his materials, and to pursue an honesty of conception, following the path of nature

The Lady of Shalott. Oil painting by John William Waterhouse, 1888

in a rationalised way and not in servile imitation. William Morris and the firm which he founded maintained close relations with the Pre-Raphaelite Brotherhood, and the following quotation from their manifesto shows how parallel were their paths: 'The Pre-Raphaelite Brotherhood has but one principle, that of absolute, uncompromising truth in all that it does, obtained by working everything down to the most minute detail from nature alone'. William Morris wanted 'honest' designs to be the privilege of every man. His was a blinkered idealism, for, regrettably, he saw the machine as an evil, as a barrier between this precious 'honesty' and the public. The romantic arty craftiness of the Arts and Crafts movement launched by Morris was the sad product of their inability to harness the machine as a tool for achieving their ends, and of their insistence on applying their principles, learnt from an idealised Medieval age, to the realities of the late nineteenth century. There are, nonetheless, many very attractive products of the Arts and Crafts movement, in many of which can be seen the seeds of Art Nouveau. Morris's textile and wallpaper designs involve elegant stylisations from nature which, if a little less restrained, would be pure Art Nouveau.

Arthur Heygate Mackmurdo founded his Century Guild in 1882, following the principles of Ruskin and Morris, and within a year had designed a chair which is, possibly, the earliest pure example of English Art Nouveau. This chair, though fairly conventional in form, has a fretwork back which characterises perfectly the principle of drawing inspiration from nature in an elegant, lively, asymmetrical abstract design which anticipates, by about fifteen years, the height of the Art Nouveau style. Ironically, many English designers who were the precursors of Art Nouveau were the most fervent in condemning the style when they saw their ideas carried to luxuriant extremes on the Continent of Europe. Walter Crane, the designer/illustrator, denied association with the 'strange decorative disease' that was gripping the Continent. Yet frequently his own designs were early tentatives in the style. In his illustration 'When lilies of the day are done and sunk the golden westering sun' (*Flora's Feast* 1889), we find the model for the *'femme-fleur'* that was to become so distinctive an Art Nouveau theme.

Both Mackmurdo and Crane exploited a rhythmic interplay of line which, when applied to the abstraction of natural forms, became one of the key features of Art Nouveau. This focus of interest on linearity and abstraction owed a good deal to the influence of Japanese art, which first manifested itself as a shaping force in Western art in the early 1860s. London had her first major confrontation with Japanese works of art when the city played host to the 1862 World Exhibition. These objects became available to collectors when Farmer & Rogers of Regent Street opened an Oriental warehouse to sell off the exhibits. The manager of this fashionable new venture was Arthur Lasenby Liberty whose store, Liberty & Co. of Regent Street, was eventually to become the leading outlet and promotional centre for English Art Nouveau. The young Liberty's clients included J. A. M. Whistler, Oscar Wilde and Edward Godwin, the first to decorate his house in Japanese style, with plain walls and clean, functional, ebonised furniture.

The Oriental influence reached the French at a slightly later

When Lilies of the day are done,
And sunk the golden westering sun.

Flora's Feast. Book illustration by Walter Crane, 1889

Silvered tea service. Dr Christopher Dresser, 1880
(*opposite*) Lithographic poster for the Ecole de Nancy. Eugène Vallin

date, though attention is always drawn to the story of the discovery by the French dealer, Félix Bracquemond, in 1856, of Japanese prints used as a wrapping-paper on goods shipped from the East. In 1862 Madame de Soye opened a shop, La Porte Chinoise, in the Rue de Rivoli, Paris; of more crucial importance, however, was the visit to the Orient in 1875 of the German-born art patron, Samuel Bing. On his return to Paris he imported and retailed the Oriental wares that had so impressed him on his travels. His clients included the brothers de Goncourt and Count Robert de Montesquiou whose passing, yet totally absorbing, interest in the arts of Japan went to the point of his dressing in Japanese costume. Bing launched a journal, *Le Japon Artistique*, in 1888, which served as a powerful mouthpiece for this advocate of Orientalism. At Nancy in Lorraine two of the leading craftsmen, Emile Gallé and Eugène Vallin, learnt to appreciate Japanese art largely as a result of a chance encounter in 1885 with Takasima, a Japanese botanist, who was a student at the Nancy École Forestière.

Two years after Bing, the English designer, Dr Christopher Dresser, made his pilgrimage to Japan, collecting objects and studying production methods. He published a lengthy account of his visit in 1882 under the title *Japan, its Architecture, Art*

Sté 3 Lorraine des Amis des Arts

Exposition d'Art Décoratif Galeries Poirel du 30 Octobre au 4 Décembre 1904

ÉCOLE de NANCY

HUMBLOT & SIMON NANCY

13

and Art Manufactures. His visit clearly influenced his style, encouraging a love of simplicity, and a fine sense of exquisitely balanced proportions. His art lay in handling the simplest of forms with the utmost sophistication. Dresser's most prophetic designs, the first pure manifestations of modernism and functionalism, date from his return from Japan. By 1899 he was being hailed in the pages of *The Studio* as '. . . perhaps the greatest of commercial designers, imposing his fantasy and invention upon the ordinary output of British industry.'

Such, then, are the elements that shaped the Art Nouveau movement as it emerged spontaneously in most of the countries of Western Europe and in the United States of America. In each country designers and artists were driven by the same impulses as they groped towards a meaningful new formula of design. One can see how the return to nature, the glorification of craftsmanship, the influence of Japanese art, and the pursuit of modernism and functionalism could conspire in varying degrees to create disparate stylistic trends. It would be wrong to obliterate the individuality of artists in any one country by trying to affix hard and fast nationalist labels. Certain obvious trends do, however, deserve comment, and two broad stylistic categories can be defined. One could call them 'hot' or 'cold' Art Nouveau, and into the first group would be placed the French, Belgian and Spanish schools. Into the second would be placed the English, but more specifically the Scottish and Austrian schools or Art Nouveau. The French were masters of the sensuous, curvilinear style. They cultivated all that was most precious, most refined and, ultimately, most bizarre and artificial. At times one almost feels sympathy for Walter Crane's misgivings (*see page* 10). The French style at its best is lush and seductive, and cannot be faulted for quality or sophistication. The Spanish architect, Antonio Gaudí, and the Belgian, Victor Horta, conceived outstanding buildings in a rich and uncompromising curvilinear style. Charles Rennie Mackintosh in Glasgow and Joseph Hoffmann and his followers in Vienna founded their style on the 'cold' interplay of horizontals and verticals, and were ultimately to prove the true pioneers of twentieth-century design.

Candleholder. Franz Hoosemans, 1910

FURNITURE

France

The perverse exuberance of French Art Nouveau found in furniture a highly satisfactory medium of expression. English purists may well have despised the lack of truth to materials, for French cabinet-makers used wood as if it were clay. Often ignoring the natural grain of the wood, they would twist and contort their material into fluid, intriguing shapes which, at their best, owed nothing to tradition but burst forth voluptuously and organically, capturing the hot-house mystery of the French 'Style 1900'.

There were two distinct centres in France, in cabinet-making as in other categories of craftsmanship, each with its characteristic features. Paris and Nancy fostered two styles, both working on a principle of returning to nature for inspiration. In Paris we find, perhaps, a more sophisticated application of this ideal. There, natural form is stylised and abstracted, the convolutions are more attenuated, more refined, and the emphasis is on a typically Parisian image of elegance. Not surprisingly one is more likely to find giltwood used in Paris, or fine woods such as the steamed pearwood favoured by Guimard.

It was the energy and enthusiasm of Emile Gallé, a man passionately fond of his native Lorraine, that created the Nancy school. Gallé, who started his career as a ceramicist before venturing first into glass then, around 1885, into furniture-making, wrote at length on the theory of furniture design and inspired other craftsmen, one of whom, Louis Majorelle, was perhaps to prove a more important cabinet-maker than Gallé.

Nancy School furniture is characterised by a provincial strength. Forms tend to be heavier and more imposing than those created in Paris. Also, the inspiration from nature was generally more direct – the structure would often be carved as a plant rather than distil the qualities of the growth of that plant. Gallé himself was the most naturalistic of designers. His love of nature led to a deep interest in woods, and for his

Mahogany *sellette* with fruitwood marquetry. Louis Majorelle, about 1900

floral or figurative marquetry work Gallé drew from a collection of about three hundred local or exotic fruitwoods, never staining them, preferring to exploit their natural qualities. Louis Majorelle and Victor Prouvé designed marquetry work under Gallé's influence. The other major characteristic of Nancy furniture was its sense of regional pride. Local plants such as the thistle, symbol of Lorraine, or cow parsley, which grew in abundance around Nancy, were employed in marquetry decoration or in full-relief carving. The sad political tug-of-war situation no doubt accentuated the Nancy designer's sense of loyalty. Gallé's patriotism is made manifest in the titles he gave to certain pieces of furniture ('meubles parlants'): for instance, a table entitled 'Je tiens au coeur de France' ('I have France in my heart'), or a desk called: 'La fôret Lorraine' ('The forest of Lorraine'), inlaid with the line from Baudelaire: 'Fôret Lorraine, tout y parlerait à l'âme en secret sa douce langue natale' ('O forests of Lorraine who would whisper to one's soul, in secret, in one's sweet native tongue').

Gallé was a great craftsman, also a great theorist and idealist, and, although his work is occasionally marred by a certain conservatism, at his best he shows great inventiveness and an almost poetic sincerity. There is a good deal of sense in the principles he sets forth. First he claims one must turn to nature and not to former styles for inspiration: limbs should follow the forms of plants, cross sections should be conceived to follow the outlines of plants and, finally, flat surfaces should reflect the craftsman's love of nature with joyful marquetry designs of landscapes or flowers.

Certain pieces of furniture signed Gallé follow the above rules. Much furniture was produced commercially in his workshops, however, which loses sight of the ideals. At the other extreme Galle's furniture becomes pure symbolism and fantasy; he conceived a bed, the head and footboards being two giant butterflies inlaid in mother-of-pearl and fruitwoods, representing dawn and twilight, and a vitrine in ironwood and lake aged oak, supported by Surrealist dragonflies in full

Tray with fruitwood marquetry. Emile Gallé, about 1900

Mahogany dressing table. Louis Majorelle, about 1900

relief, their eyes in blown *clair de lune* glass. Dragonflies or bats swarm over cabinets or tables; glass insects crawl over marquetry foliage.

Louis Majorelle's furniture is sculptural rather than anecdotal. Brought up as a cabinet-maker, Majorelle was clearly imbued with a sense of French tradition and a feeling for fine proportions. He constantly emphasises the importance of the basic lines of any piece of furniture: 'The first need is to seek a healthy structure capable of inspiring a sense of harmony, and such that the essential lines should have an architectural sense of proportion . . . The craftsman must ensure that the lines can exist without decoration . . . The richness of a piece of furniture should owe nothing to a surfeit of decoration – elegant lines and handsome proportions should suffice.'

The appeal of Majorelle's furniture is more direct than that of Gallé's. Majorelle, working usually in hard mahogany, succeeded in giving a free and fluid sculptural quality to his designs. The feet and legs of the dressing table illustrated, for example, create a liquid pattern of sensuous returning curves; the *sellette* has a lively springiness achieved by the emphatic lines of the bowed legs. The former piece is enhanced by floral whiplash bronze drawer handles and a key in the form of a stem of cow parsley, the *sellette* by a marquetry pattern of leaves; yet the insistence is very much on the shape and not on any significance with which that shape may be laden. Majorelle's finest work is the series of salon, bedroom and bureau suites which he designed between 1900 and about 1906, decorated with lilies or orchids in gilt bronze. After 1906 there was a marked decline in the aesthetic quality of his production and the tendency was towards heaviness. Two other Nancy designers deserve mention. Eugène Vallin and Jacques Gruber both worked in similar vein, creating heavily sculpted forms depending not on decoration but on organic interplay of line. When one observes the lines of the *sellette* by Vallin illustrated, it comes as no surprise to learn that, with his architectural training and interest in mass, he was amongst the first to experiment in France with poured concrete buildings.

Oak *sellette*. Eugène Vallin, about 1900

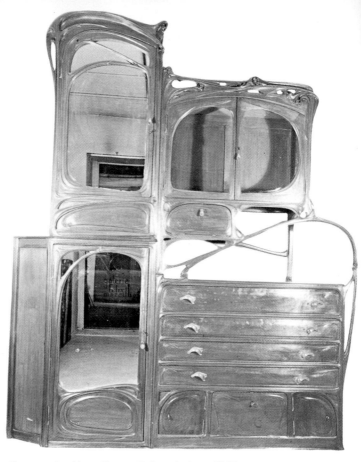

Pearwood cabinet. Hector Guimard, about 1900

Paris

Paris, as we have already seen, created a highly refined school of furniture designers. A great patron was Samuel Bing, whose shop, L'Art Nouveau, in the Rue de Provence, was to give the style its name. He promoted the talents of young designers by selling their work, also by organising exhibitions. Under his wing, three designers in particular were able to expose their ideas at the Great 1900 Paris Exhibition. Eugène Colonna created a salon, Eugène Gaillard a bedroom and dining room, whilst Georges de Feure conceived a dressing room and boudoir, essentially feminine rooms where he could play his refinement to maximum effect. De Feure used delicate gilt-wood, pastel damasks or silks embroidered with Symbolist scenes of *femmes fatales* strolling with attenuated greyhounds. His work has been described as 'a hymn to the beauty of women'.

An apparently isolated genius, whose furniture is perhaps conceptually the most far-reaching of all that created in Paris or Nancy, was Hector Guimard. Here was an architect who saw it as his duty to create complete environments. Any building which he designed would be conceived organically with furniture, internal woodwork, lock plates, light fittings, and so forth, all considered as essential parts of the structure. This explains the impression of abnormality created by certain items of furniture by Guimard when taken out of context. Pieces were designed to fill corners at odd angles, or to sweep over doors, or fireplaces. Paris was first brought face to face with Guimard when his bizarre hybrids, the plant-like Métro entrances in green painted cast iron, sprouted in 1900. The English, typically, were even less appreciative of his work than the French. A *1908 Studio Year Book* article comments – 'The fancy, the imprévu and the superabundant imagination of M. Hector Guimard caused him to oscillate almost simultaneously between fascinating success and disconcerting error'. Today we are able to perceive the importance of Guimard's works. He was not a cabinet-maker drawing his inspiration from nature, but a sculptor in wood who, having assimilated the essential principle of natural growth, was able to toy with line and mass. He created fluid, asymmetrical sculptural forms, whose earlier emphatically linear, or later softly palpitating, qualities went beyond naturalism, and anticipated Abstract Expressionism.

England and Scotland

One British artist bears comparison in the quality and significance of his visions with Hector Guimard. Charles Rennie Mackintosh, the Glasgow architect/designer, preached an aestheticism as pure as Guimard's, an aestheticism more spartan, less Baroque, than the Frenchman's, and perhaps more

Lampshade, plated brass and coloured glass, about 1900
(*opposite*) Chair and table. Charles Rennie Mackintosh, about 1901–2

truly pioneering. For whilst Guimard was indulging his self-engulfing decadence, Mackintosh was exploring the possibilities of clean, crisp interplays of horizontals and verticals, of shapes that could ultimately be adapted to mass-production – his was not an élitist art – though he was no great business-man, and never really harnessed his talent to democratic manufacture.

Charles Rennie Mackintosh was born in Glasgow, and was, no doubt, imbued with the city's character during his years as an apprentice architect or student at the School of Art. The tradition of Scottish Baronial architecture is an important element in his work.

With a fellow architectural draughtsman, J. Herbert MacNair, he attended classes at the Glasgow School of Art, and there they met the Macdonald sisters who were shortly

to become their wives. The 'Glasgow Four', as they were affectionately known, or 'The Spook School', as they were less amicably described, tackled every aspect of applied art. With Mackintosh as the guiding light, and as their architect, they created complete environments in a very personal and highly stylised expression of the Art Nouveau mood.

This Glasgow School style, with its willowy attenuation, the frequent starkness and its agonised, emaciated, decorative figures, was too extreme for the general English public. Mackintosh and his colleagues found great sympathy in Vienna, where the Secessionists were experimenting with a comparably 'modernist' style, and he found sympathy with a few inspired patrons in Scotland. The most notable of these was Miss Cranston, a Glasgow tea-house proprietor who commissioned Mackintosh to design a series of tea-rooms between 1897 and 1912. The sophisticated furniture which Mackintosh designed for these rooms, together with the furniture he conceived for a number of his private houses, must rank among the highest achievements of British Art Nouveau. His versatility can be seen in the contrast between the spartan lines of one of his dark oak chairs and the preciousness and refinement of his white, highback chairs with their restrained touches of heliotrope.

Charles Annesley Voysey was, like Mackintosh, an architect who designed furniture and furnishings. He worked in England designing attractive private houses, and the furniture he created for these was a milder version of the bold ideas expressed by Mackintosh. Voysey's furniture is simple, uncluttered, and appealing in its directness. Baillie Scott was, similarly, a domestic architect who created the complete environment, but his furniture tends to be a little too whimsical and romantic with its mock-rustic details. Ernest Gimson combined simplicity and functionalism with fine workmanship – this was the exception rather than the rule in English cabinet-making. Finally, one should mention Liberty & Co. who were instrumental in popularising a certain type of furniture which attempted too often to compromise between British and Continental ideas.

Oak dresser, Liberty & Co.

SCULPTURE

The cult of Woman was a prominent symptom of the *fin-de-siècle* hunger for imagery. And the cult created images as unhealthy as the desires which fed on them. For the decadence and spiritual unrest prevalent towards the turn of the century led men's minds, in desperation, down extreme and insecure paths of fantasy. This element of disquiet had entered the heroines of pictorial art with the Pre-Raphaelite beauties of Burne-Jones and Millais and the more exaggerated, neurotic images of Rossetti. These solemn-featured creatures with their characteristic strong jaws, broad nostrils, heavy dark eyes, and fiery waved hair, clearly reflect, as mirrors, the torments of their creators. Philippe Jullian, the critic, traces their evolution from the sad sensuality of Rossetti's models to the cadaverous type in vogue at the end of the century. In France, Gustave Moreau was the first to convey strong undercurrents of psychic disruption in his symbol-laden canvasses of pagan queens in quazi-Byzantine splendour. As the ideal evolved in two dimensions towards the drugged desperation of, say, Klimt's *Salomé*, or the pale tragedy of Fernand Khnopff's frozen beauties, so authors conveyed the imagery in their writings. Baudelaire's ideal was 'Sois belle et sois triste'. Wilde reached a high pitch of neurosis in his *Salomé*, and wrote a poem to the Sphinx, symbol of impenetrable, omnipotent

Bronze *vide-poches*. French, about 1900

(*opposite*) *Ophelia* by Maurice Bouval. Gilt-bronze

female mystery. The essential impotence which is at the root of the escapist, yet stifling, hot-house character of decadent Art Nouveau found a kind of necrophiliac gratification in the cult of the morbid and moribund Ophelia, or a kind of sanctity at the altar of the all-devouring quasi-mystical 'Femme 1900'.

To appreciate Art Nouveau sculpture is first to appreciate the symbolism with which artists loaded their work. Before considering this in detail, however, one might first note that during the Art Nouveau years sculpture acquired a special significance. We have seen how one of the important ideals of Art Nouveau theorists was to destroy what were considered the purely arbitrary barriers between 'fine' and 'applied' arts. As a result, sculpture was treated as a decorative craft and there was a vogue for small domestic-size works which broke the barrier by being conceived as lamps, ashtrays, pen-trays, bell-pushes, or paper weights. There evolved also a fashion for 'crafted' or multi-media sculpture incorporating ivory or semi-precious stones, or details of enamel work which was more the work of a jeweller than a sculptor.

There was a kind of reversal of rôles during the Art Nouveau years. For just as we have seen Guimard elevating furniture to the level of traditional sculpture, so we see the sculptors of the period making theirs a decorative art.

Many sculptors exploited the small decorative bronze as a three-dimensional expression of *fin-de-siècle* moods. Their work was evidently successful, for the better quality examples were much imitated to reach a wider public, and many poor quality mass-produced works survive in base metals such as spelter or pewter. The Germans were possibly the largest commercial manufacturers of debased Art Nouveau sculpture. The Württembergische Metallwarenfabrik borrowed from France the typical dreamy-eyed maiden with her long flowing hair and swirling drapes, and adapted her to adorn mirror frames, trays, jugs, even walking-cane handles in silvered pewter further decorated with trite asymmetrical floral motifs or with weak whiplashes.

The English had no school of Art Nouveau sculpture. They were more concerned, towards the turn of the century,

Le Secret by Pierre-Félix Fix-Masseau. Gilt-bronze, before 1897

31

Cléo de Mérode by Louis Chalon. Gilt-bronze, 1900

with following the tradition of the New Sculpture of the 1880s, or were immersed in an elaborate and romantic Medievalism typified in Gilbert's resplendent knights.

Austria fostered one bronze sculptor of note, Gustav Gurschner, who showed imagination in designing lamps, their shades of Loetz lustre glass, or nautilus shells supported on stylised waves before bronze maidens, their bodies terminating in bold Art Nouveau arabesques. A bronze hand mirror, its handle a mermaid supporting the mirror in her outstretched arms and gazing at her own reflection, is a typically inventive conceit.

France produced the most consistently imaginative sculpture, and some of the best quality Art Nouveau bronzes bear

Gilt and silvered bronze bust for Houbigant. Alphonse Mucha, 1900

Paris foundry marks. The firms Susse Frères and Siot-Décauville cast and put their stamp on the work of some of the most prominent artists of the day. Jean Dampt and Julien Caussé were both notable for their mixed-media work. Dampt is perhaps best known for his celebrated group of a silvered knight embracing an ivory, jewel-encrusted maiden. Caussé is best known for his *La Fée des Glaces*, an ice-maiden in cold, silvered metal standing on an iceberg of crackled glass attributed to Ernest Léveillé. Théodore Rivière was another who attempted mixed-media work. His figures and groups tend to be seeped in the symbolism of Middle Eastern legend. Agathon Leonard, Charles Korschann and Leo Laporte-Blairsy deserve mention for their bronze or gilt-bronze lamps or table decorations.

Leonard is known for a crisply modelled series, *Le Jeu de l'écharpe*, edited in gilt-bronze by Siot-Décauville around 1900 and representing the various stages of a dance, loosely inspired by Loïe Fuller. Leo Laporte-Blairsy designed lamps modelled as women holding caskets, or giant flowers which conceal the light fittings.

The bronze bust illustrated, *Ophélia*, is by Maurice Bouval and is a very direct expression of the ideal of Woman discussed earlier. This sculpture has a delicious limp and liquid sensuality as well as an appealing quality of mystery. What secrets lie dormant behind those heavily lidded eyes? Surely the secret which haunts Bouval's *Ophélia* is the same as that which disturbs Pierre-Félix Fix-Masseau's gilt-bronze figure, *Le Secret*. Her scarcely concealed distress clearly involves a mystery whose explanation is sealed forever within the symbolic casket which she clutches to her chest. Her ritualistic pose, her nakedness revealed through the mannered drapes of her cloak, and the inexplicable star of David on her pedestal, add to the symbolism.

An important aspect of Art Nouveau sculpture was this expression of mystery; equally significant was the attempt to express movement. The asymmetrical flowing line was one of the most salient features of the Art Nouveau style, and artists experimenting with curves were, understandably, totally captivated by certain dancers whose movements became the living embodiment of the style. Loïe Fuller and Cléo de Mérode, who were both at their peak in their performance at the great Paris Exhibition of 1900, are possibly the best known of these. The studies of Loïe Fuller by Raoul Larche and Pierre Roche were the finest of countless efforts to capture her qualities in bronze. Louis Chalon's gilt-bronze figure of Cléo de Mérode presents the dancer as the embodiment of the Spirit of 1900, and is an unusually healthy variation on the theme of the cult of Woman. She stands, proud, but not arrogant, with the light of the new century blazing optimistically from her brow.

The Paris Exhibition of 1900 was in many ways the crowning moment of the French Art Nouveau style. The style had started to emerge seriously towards the mid 1890s and this

Gilt and silvered bronze bust. Alphonse Mucha, 1900

Exhibition gathered together the work of the foremost designers of the day at a moment when they were practised, but while their work still retained a quality of freshness and excitement. Within five or ten years Art Nouveau motifs had become insensitively abused, the good ideas bastardised by plagiarists, and many designers were showing a tendency towards heaviness, having lost the inspiration and tension of their earlier work. This Paris Exhibition, at which La Loïe and Cléo de Mérode triumphed, was virtually the first and the last great showing and, in certain cases, had a dual effect of inspiring as well as promoting. One artist, best known for his lithographic work, was inspired by commissions for the Exhibition to turn his talent to sculpture. Alphonse Mucha, the Czech artist who immortalised Sarah Bernhardt in his two-dimensional work, created few bronzes, but these few are amongst the greatest achievements of Art Nouveau sculpture. In his diary Mucha speaks of two of these, for both of which he was awarded bronze medals: 'I was busy modelling the statue of Bosnia and Herzegovina. I had another statue to make for the Houbigant exposition. The perfumer was a friend of mine and I promised it to him unaware that I would be so hard pressed for time. It was a bust of a woman, gilded and crowned with a diadem.' All that survives of the first mentioned is an old studio photograph of the maquette. The Houbigant bust was rediscovered in 1970. This is the small bust illustrated, her eyes downcast enigmatically, her hair and diadem formalised to the point where they become an iconography in themselves. The Paris Exhibition catalogues list a further bronze, *La Nature* by Mucha, though it is still uncertain to which sculpture this title refers. A recent discovery was a bronze by Mucha sculpted for the 1900 Exhibition as a study for a vast project, *Le Pavillon de L'Homme*. This was a scheme for a vast orb-like building in semi-Art Nouveau, semi-Byzantine style, taller than the Eiffel Tower and destined to house a display showing the history, evolution and achievement of Man. This gargantuan fantasy was never realised, was never more than sketches or models, but Mucha did model studies for the mammoth corner figures. This surviving bronze is one such study, and, in its affinities with the new school of sculpture fathered by Rodin, is a departure from

Female nude by Alphonse Mucha. Bronze, 1899–1900

Mucha's usual style. Mucha's most impressive sculpture is the almost life-size bust of a young woman cast in 1900, and probably destined for the Paris Exhibition. A contemporary photograph shows the bust with what resembles a light-bulb in the crest of the coronet and a pierced hole at the base which could be an opening for an electric lead, suggesting that this might have been another shining tribute to the new century. The idea of a bare bulb crowning a sculpture would not have been unattractive to a generation for whom electricity was still a novelty. In this young woman, with her long hair, flowing in formalised arabesques around her breasts to form a base, and with that *fin-de-siècle*, indefinable, melancholic beauty in her solemn face, Mucha combines a lively graphic strength with sincere sensitivity.

GLASS

France

That glass should be treated as a substance which was by definition translucent and colourless was the first myth to be shattered by Art Nouveau glass-makers. In their hands, glass became something quite new, quite special: it took on the qualities of semi-precious stones, it was speckled, veined, or marbled, given a rich opaque metallic lustre, was made dense, muted and mysterious, or thick and treacly with a waxy tactile appeal.

In the greatest achievements of Art Nouveau glass-makers, we find expressed the first and most essential principles of Art Nouveau design. Firstly, that form and decoration should be one, and secondly, that the merits of any piece should be contained within the very materials employed, and should in no way appear as additions or afterthoughts.

Art Nouveau glass had a few great masters and their many imitators. Perhaps the greatest was Emile Gallé, though Louis Comfort Tiffany must rank high for his quality and inventiveness. Emile Gallé we have already encountered as a cabinet-maker. This was a secondary interest, though, and he undoubtedly found his happiest medium of expression in glass. Gallé was born on the 4th May, 1846, at Nancy. His father, Charles Gallé, a prosperous designer and manufacturer of ceramics and director of the Faïencerie de Saint Clément, had a shop in Nancy selling glassware made at Meisenthal in the Saar valley in addition to the ceramics he produced. Emile was brought up designing imitation eighteenth-century decorative ceramics, but his interest turned to glass, and, after initial experimental phases during the late 1870s and the 80s, he broke new ground technically and won considerable acclaim.

Gallé's first phase is known as the 'transparent phase'. During the late 1870s and well into the 80s, he worked in clear glass, occasionally tinted blue, more frequently tinted a pale amber. Form and decoration were still very much inspired by traditional Islamic or Venetian types which Gallé had studied. The decoration at this time was enamelled, often in thick relief,

Enamelled glass scent bottle and stopper. Emile Gallé, 1890s

A collection of glassware by Emile
Gallé. Carved cameo and
marqueterie-de-verre work,
about 1900

and in charming colours. Surfaces were made more interesting with gilding, acid-texturing or with the application of glass cabochons. Already, though, one can sense Gallé's love of nature, for these early pieces began to incorporate delightful dragonflies, bizarre insects and a rich and always accurate flora. Also making itself apparent at this early stage was a certain Oriental feeling. Japan was to be a great source of inspiration for Art Nouveau designers, and Gallé's decorative draughtsmanship betrays this influence. An Oriental influence can perhaps be traced in the technical affinities between Gallé's later cameo glass and Chinese cased glassware.

One off-shoot of Gallé's transparent phase was his *clair de lune* glass, an opalescent glass which acquired a brilliant sapphire tint when held up to the light.

The year 1889 proved something of a stepping stone for Gallé, for it was at the Paris Exhibition of that year that he first showed his *verre double*. These were vases, blown in one coloured glass, then cased in one or more layers of glass of different colours. After painting a floral design in acid-resistant wax in positive, the casing would be etched away leaving the design standing in relief. The process could be repeated to achieve further tonal subtlety. Finer quality cameo pieces would be carved by Gallé or his craftsmen on the wheel. Hand-carving allowed for considerable subtlety in the gradation of tone or colour, and also left an attractive waxy, minutely faceted and gently polished surface, considerably more appealing than the dull, rough and frosty texture left by the acid. Within the category of Gallé's cameo work the subdivisions are limitless, for the production was vast and uneven (by 1904, the year of Gallé's death, his workshops employed about three hundred craftsmen making the popular cameo glass, as well as commercial repeats of Gallé's earlier enamelled glass). Certain acid-etched pieces were enhanced by fire-polishing, others were part etched then finished on the wheel. Crude cameo vases, drab in colour and poor in execution, were made long after Gallé's death, and by sheer force of numbers have tended to misrepresent the name they bear. Gallé conceived a series of acid cameo vases in very high relief. These are his

Marqueterie-de-verre onion vase. Emile Gallé, 1900

mould-blown vases, often involving designs of ripe fruit, a subject well suited to the possibilities of the technique. The colours and finish associated with these vases, however, are not exciting.

The year 1897 saw the introduction of Gallé's most exciting technique, *marqueterie-de-verre*. The process can be compared to marquetry work on furniture. Unlike the cameo vases, the design does not stand in relief but is made up of pieces of semi-molten glass embedded into the surface of the glass body while it is still warm and soft. The design would be finished with wheel-carving when cold, but the application of the colours required speed, and tremendous skill and control, for the body would have to be constantly re-heated. Many cracked in the making. Good *marqueterie-de-verre* pieces nearly always bear Gallé's personal signature – cut in with a fine point in spindly letters.

Marqueterie-de-verre pieces generally have a marvellous feeling of spontaneity, which is accentuated by the fact that the semi-molten glass is generally pressed, not into a plain glass body, but into a fluid, textured glass body with swirling internal blown decoration of coloured streaks or of fine bubbles. The onion vase illustrated is a fine example both of *marqueterie-de-verre* and of Gallé's fascination with describing nature: his motto, carved over the doorway of his workshop, was 'Ma racine est au fond des bois' ('My roots are in the depths of the woods'). Gallé has here achieved a superb freedom in the blowing of the glass body, with its flame-like inclusions licking up towards the rim, and the inside cased in rich, syrupy cyclamen; at the same time we see great control in the inlaying of the fine green stems, in the gutsy carving of the brown onion skin, and in the blowing of the finely threaded foot. More important perhaps is the conception of the piece, expressing as it does all the qualities and facets of the onion, from the burst of slender roots, through the uneven layers of outer skin up to the onion flowers.

Gallé clearly saw himself as a kind of three-dimensional poet. In his personal creations, either in marqueterie glass, or in his unrestrained sculpted and applied glass, he set out to express

Glass vase with gilt bronze mounts. Daum Frères, about 1900

Pâte-de-verre pot and cover. Amalric Walter, about 1910

the moods and ideas of the Symbolist poets whom he admired so much. Many of his finer pieces were inspired by specific lines from the poems of Baudelaire, or Hugo, which Gallé would then inscribe in the glass body.

Of all the glass-makers to be influenced by Gallé, perhaps the most important were the brothers Auguste et Antonin Daum. Their father, Jean Daum, had, in 1875, acquired a glass factory in Nancy, the Verrerie de Nancy. As in the workshop operated by Gallé's father, the most important production was of decorative table and domestic ware. So impressed were the Daum Brothers with the work exhibited by Gallé at Paris in 1889 where they were fellow exhibitors, that they soon turned their energy to the production of art glass.

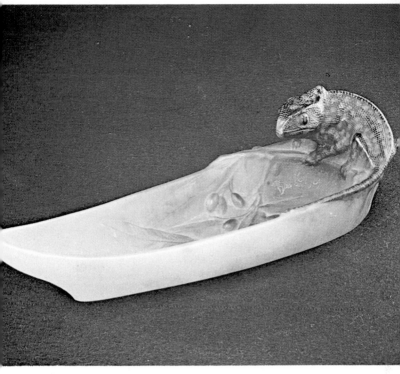

Pâte-de-verre dish. Amalric Walter, about 1910

Their commercial production of cameo glass can be closely compared with Gallé's, though they were distinctive in their use of mottled glass bodies or of gilt and enamelled decoration on acid-cut vases. The Daum Brothers showed particular skill in their use of the engraver's wheel on good quality cameo work. Occasionally, a little of Gallé's genius can be felt reflected in their work. The vase illustrated is a good example of a carved piece that has a touch of inspiration in its conception. This vase is a kind of symbolic pagan ritual vessel, with its band of thorns reflecting the blue thorns in the glass, and its grail-like base set with cabochons. The glass tear drops have acquired a sinister anecdotal significance.

The Muller Brothers of Lunéville were similarly influenced

by Gallé, with whom they had trained before establising their own glassworks. Their production was generally of a fairly commercial standard, though certain good carved vases bear their signature. D. Christian Meisenthal is a signature found on cameo glass in the Gallé manner and of quite a high standard. D'Argental, Richard, Arsall and Delatte are signatures found on rather uninspired imitative work.

Gallé's influence spread to Paris, where Auguste Legras produced rather drab enamelled or cameo landscape or floral vases. In Paris, Le Verre Français also produced crude commercial acid-cut glass.

The imitators of Emile Gallé deserve little credit. More worthy is the contribution of a group of glass-makers whose efforts to find new ways of using glass led to independent technical innovations. Particularly successful was the Art Nouveau revival of the ancient skill of casting glass paste. The French called it *pâte-de-verre* (glass paste), and the technique consisted in crushing glass into a fine powder, mixing in a little water to make a paste, and adding metallic oxides to provide colour after the firing. This paste would be packed into a mould made from a wax model, and would be fired in a kiln at a high temperature. The paste took on colour and fired into a dense opaque mass with a frosty, sugary surface.

Henri Cros was the first to work in this technique. His subjects are generally Classical in inspiration, and the roughness

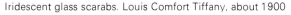

Iridescent glass scarabs. Louis Comfort Tiffany, about 1900

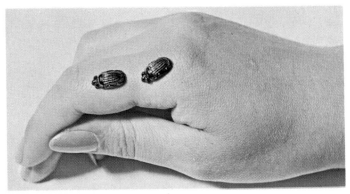

of texture of his work and the lack of contrast in the colouring bear witness to his rôle as an early experimenter. Various craftsmen evolved refinements to the technique. By adding an adhesive to the paste, for example, it was found possible to take a piece from its mould before firing, and so add to the quality by detailed modelling with a spatula. It was found that if a vase was left to cool slowly over a period of days, a higher degree of clarity could be achieved. Names associated with the process are the Daum Brothers, who then became concessioners for Amalric Walter, one of the most inventive *pâte-de-verre* designers, Décorchemont, Dammousse and Despret.

Louis Comfort Tiffany

The ancient Egyptian references implicit in the lustre glass scarabs illustrated make a good starting point in a study of the glassware made by the American, Louis Comfort Tiffany. For this artist's introduction to glass took place on a series of visits to North Africa and the Middle East during the late 1860s and 1870s. He formed a collection of ancient glassware and was deeply fascinated by it on various counts. The freedom of form, an often unintentional asymmetry or irregularity, seemed appealing at a time when designers were trying to escape from stifling conventions. More especially, however, Tiffany was captivated by the wonderful colouring and textures of this ancient glass. Centuries of lying buried had caused the glass to decompose, and metallic oxides in the soil gave to the flaking surfaces a delicate and fascinating nacreous iridescence, in the palest shades of blue/green and gold. In Cyprus, Tiffany found vases that had been given an attractive, rough, gritty, pitted surface by decomposition. In the Middle East, he learnt to appreciate glass canework decoration. It was the essential integrity of this glass that so attracted Tiffany, and, although he was never aligned by any dogma to the Art Nouveau movement, he did become involved in the search for new forms, and in the insistence on sympathy with materials. Samuel Bing, a great admirer of Tiffany's art, pointed out significantly that 'if we are called upon to declare the supreme characteristic of this glassware, we would say that it resides in the fact that the means employed for the purpose of ornamentation are sought and found in the vitreous substance itself, without the use of

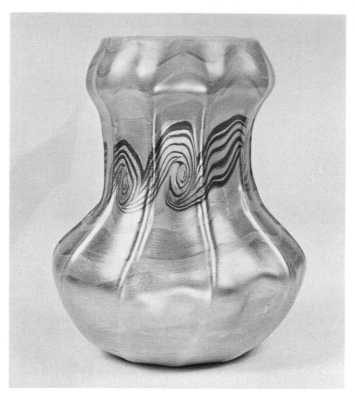

Gold lustre glass vase inlaid with red glass. Louis Comfort Tiffany, about 1900

either brush, wheel or acid. When cool, the article is finished'.

Tiffany's first experiments with glass-making were for decorative tiles and panels to complement the interiors created by his firm, the Associated Artists. He soon forgot about the interiors to devote himself exclusively to his glass production, for which he found a large and eager market. As in the case of Emile Gallé, the tremendous demand and the resulting expansion of the artist's workshops meant that output must be considered in two categories. Firstly, the less interesting commercial wares, which in the case of Tiffany meant his rather harsh gold iridescent decorative tableware; and secondly, the smaller proportion of fine quality experimental pieces made either by the artist or under his close supervision. Tiffany wares can be fairly easily categorised. The largest group, as we have seen, comprises his plain gold lustre glass. The second, still semi-commercial, group consists of gold or blue lustre pieces bearing a certain amount of decoration, perhaps a few inlaid tendrils or coloured veining. This group can be extended to include more subtly decorated pieces which are amongst Tiffany's finest creations. These are the beautiful veined flower-form vases or elaborate peacock feather pieces which won Tiffany such acclaim. His admirer, Samuel Bing, helps us to appreciate their quality as he describes their creation:

'Look at the incandescent ball of glass as it comes out of the furnace; it is slightly dilated by an initial inspiration of air. The workman charges it at certain pre-arranged points with small quantities of glass, of different textures and different colours, and in this operation is hidden the germ of the intended ornamentation. The little ball is then returned to the fire to be heated. Again it is subjected to a similar treatment (the process being sometimes repeated as many as twenty times), and, when all the different glasses have been combined and manipulated in different ways, and the article has been brought to its definite state as to form and dimensions, it presents the following appearance: The *motifs* introduced into the ball when it was small have grown with the vase itself, but in differing proportions; they have lengthened or broadened out, while each tiny ornament fills the place assigned to it in advance in the mind of the artist.' (Reprinted from *Artistic America, Tiffany Glass, and Art Nouveau* by Samuel Bing. By permission of the MIT Press, Cambridge, Mass. Copyright 1970 by the Massachusetts Institute of Technology.)

The red and gold vase illustrated is a good example of the process detailed above. It is further enhanced by bearing an engraved number prefixed with 'O', which indicates a special order and by the inclusion of red glass, which is one of the rarest Tiffany colours. Tiffany worked in other techniques. Some claim his paper-weight vases with their superb millefiori details as his best pieces. Others lay emphasis on those pieces which imitate stones – Tiffany's marbleised glass or Agate ware. Of undisputed importance, however, are his 'Cypriote' and 'Lava' vases, the former olive green or brown, and with the irregular gritty texture of ancient vases studied on his travels, the latter usually in gold on blue glass and having the appearance of dripping lava. These sensitive, abstract forms are deliberately non-figurative, deliberately non-symbolist.

We should be grateful to Art Nouveau glass-makers for their practice of signing their glassware. Tiffany glass almost invariably bears his engraved initials L.C.T. or his full name, with or without the trade name 'favrile' (from an old English word meaning made by hand), and certain pieces retain their original paper labels. It was doubtless a pride in his work that led Tiffany to sign his glassware. Perhaps, also, it was to avoid his imitators, and they were numerous, taking his market. One rival manufacturer of lustre glass caused Tiffany particular concern, and he insisted that, whenever their glass was sold alongside his, it should be signed by its creator. This was the Austrian firm of Loetz Witwe.

The Loetz factory in Klostermühle came under the control of Johann Loetz in 1830 and when he died in 1848 his widow took over the management. The workshop kept the name Loetz Witwe (i.e. widow), though it was under the direction of Johann's grandson, Max von Spaun, that the firm won international acclaim after his accession in 1879. Prizes were won in Brussels in 1888, and in Paris the following year. When Von Spaun started his experiments with iridescent glassware (one of Tiffany's workers defected and gave away precious secrets to him), and shrewdly used Bing's Paris shop as an outlet, great success followed. Indeed, only two years after Loetz had patented their process they shared a *Grand Prix* at the Paris Exhibition of 1900 alongside Daum, Gallé and Tiffany.

Loetz forms are rarely exciting, the interest is more in the quality of the lustre. One finds blue, green and gold lustres, or subtle yellow or toffee tones in splashed or trailed patterns, and on occasion, finely feathered vases in the Tiffany manner. Loetz added silver overlays to certain pieces, the whiplash lines of the silver acting as a crisp foil to the silky iridescence. Loetz creations never surpassed Tiffany in inventiveness or daring, but were often richly decorative in their own right.

Feathered lustre glass vase. Loetz, about 1900

The Loetz glassworks acted as host to various Austrian glass-makers. This has led to confusion over the attribution of certain categories of Austrian glass, and has, sadly, brought Loetz into disrepute. Professor Rudolf Bakalowitz of Graz made iridescent glassware, distinctive for its fine, regular, combed lustre festoons, usually in green and gold and in uninspired forms. Joseph Palme König made crude versions of the typical Loetz vases as well as a large number of vases in dark blue or amethyst with applied glass trailing in the same colour. The German glass-maker, Karl Koepping, deserves acclaim for his pure Art Nouveau flower-form vases. These follow the principle of form being decoration, and consist of flowers blown in full relief and supported on glass stems and with glass leaves of an attenuated fragility that even Tiffany did not dare.

British Glass

In England and Scotland the turn of the century was not a great period for glass-making. English cameo glass of the Victorian period, by such great names as George Woodall, marked a high point, and the Art Nouveau years were comparatively infertile. One firm, however, James Couper & Sons of Glasgow, with the intervention of the ubiquitous Dr Christopher Dresser, saved the picture from being entirely gloomy. They launched a range of glassware which achieved popularity during the 1890s under its trade name 'Clutha', this being an old Scottish word for cloudy. Dresser states that 'glass has a molten state in which it can be blown into the most beautiful of shapes . . . this process is the work of but a few seconds' and he begs that the material be worked 'in its most simple and befitting manner'. He created sensual elongated and gently constricted globular shapes, usually in a pale green glass 'clouded' with internal swirls of milky glass, bubbles or aventurine. Dresser was able to achieve a freedom comparable with that of Tiffany's pieces, and was also able to display the superb control of the vase illustrated, with its rich and mellow amber body and finely inlaid feathering of opaque olive glass.

'Clutha' glass vase. Dr Christopher Dresser, 1890s

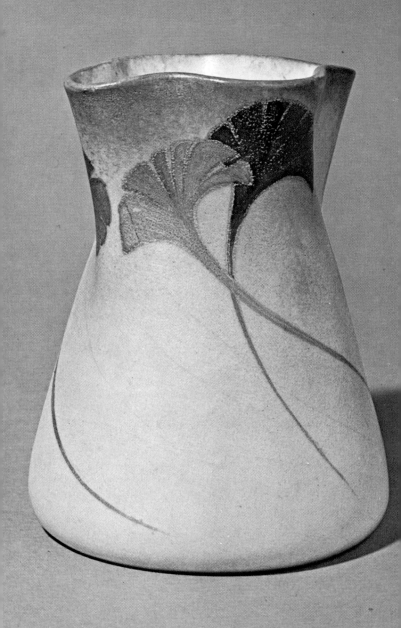

CERAMICS

Porcelain was introduced to the European market in the early eighteenth century. This new material was revered almost as the eighth wonder of the world, and important national workshops created truly delightful wares, finely modelled and exquisitely gilt and decorated. France and Germany were the leading manufacturers. During the nineteenth century these same national workshops were largely content to rework patterns and ideas that had already proved themselves so successful. As a result, the experimental urge weakened, and the porcelain and ceramic industries became complacent, their *tours de force* becoming more a question of exaggeration than of innovation.

During the last quarter of the nineteenth century, however, a new generation of craftsmen emerged, artist potters interested in the technical possibilities of their medium, keen to explore new glazes, new textures and new colours. Instrumental in the re-awakening of these craftsmen to the fascinations of their materials was the influx during the second half of the nineteenth century of Oriental ceramics. The extensive range of colours that the Chinese or Japanese were able to achieve on high-fired wares put Europeans to shame. Similarly the purity of form and integrity of decoration of early Oriental ceramics at once shamed and inspired potters who now felt the need to escape convention and to create ceramics that were above all 'honest', neither trying to imitate forms better suited to bronze or silver, nor with any other decoration than their own glazed surface.

They have been given the collective title of 'Studio' potters, and their rôle in applying the principles of Art Nouveau to ceramics is of prime importance. Following the tendency towards a freedom of form, they modelled vegetabloid or entirely abstract shapes which can verge almost on the obscene with their oozing sensual contours; and, following the policy of truth to materials, they sought decorative interest, as far as possible, only in the form and texture of their wares. The medium once again was the message. Studio potters

Glazed pottery vase. Clément Massier, about 1900

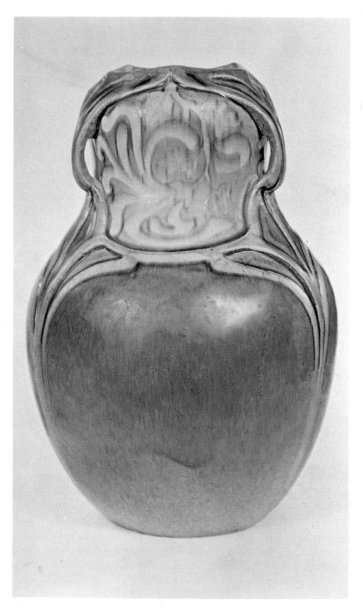

Glazed stoneware *coupe*. Paul Gauguin and Ernest Chaplet, 1887–8
(*opposite*) Glazed pottery vase. Edmond Lachenal, about 1900

often deliberately worked in 'rough' materials. Stoneware or earthenware were in favour and the aim was good craftsmanship and quality, but not a superficial 'salon' sophistication. Porcelain was relatively neglected by the new potters, though certain exquisite Art Nouveau creations survive, most notable being the Dutch Rozenburg ware. The craze was for earthenwares, and certain French potters were amongst the first to make headway. Theodore Deck, Auguste Delaherche and Ernest Chaplet were keen pioneers, and of these the name of Chaplet enjoys a particular glamour, perhaps as a result of his collaboration with Paul Gauguin.

Ernest Chaplet, born in 1835, was introduced to ceramics before the age of twenty. His vocation led him through various phases of experimentation until by the mid 80s he had mastered high-fired techniques and produced good *sang-de-boeuf* glazes. He went from strength to strength during the 80s and 90s, taking a gold medal at the Paris Universal Exhi-

Gourd vase in salt-glazed stoneware. The Martin Brothers, 1910

bition of 1889 and triumphing at the Paris Exhibition of 1900,
and all the time devising new textures and colours. When
failing eyesight forced him to abandon his craft, a last firing
consumed all his records and zealously protected glaze
secrets. It was in the winter of 1886–7 that Chaplet fired a
series of pieces modelled or decorated in strong proto-Art
Nouveau style by Gauguin. The dish illustrated, in stoneware
with an irregular dripped glaze and of very free modelling, is
referred to in a letter from Gauguin to Odilon Redon: . . .

notably a cup which I consider a rare piece because of the difficulty of firing and the chances of collapsing in the heat'. The piece is interesting for its association; also, of course, for its quality and its Art Nouveau feeling in the free-flying lily tendrils, and in the melting quality of the handle as it scrolls down to the irregular feet. A large number of other French potters deserve mention. Adrien-Pierre Dalpayrat and Emile Decoeur, Jean Carriès and Edmond Lachenal were particularly talented. In the South of France, at Golfe Juan, Clément Massier worked on lustre glazes, with Art Nouveau floral motifs shimmering in shades ranging from peacock to deep olives and burgundies. The Symbolist painter, Lucien Lévy-Dhurmer, managed the Massier studios for a number of years and showed a particular interest in decorating lustrewares. The muted autumnal colours and wistful trailed plant motifs on the Massier vase illustrated are characteristic of the languid French hot-house Art Nouveau style, treated with a Japanese graphic restraint.

It would be misleading to assume that all French turn-of-the-century ceramics were obstinately pursuing the 'Studio' and 'craft' image and there are notable examples of porcelain wares more traditional in concept. Bing, who was instrumental in spreading an understanding of Japanese art in France, commissioned Georges de Feure and Eugène Colonna to design elegant decorative porcelain tableware. These pieces are underglaze-coloured with pastel Art Nouveau floral or linear motifs on a white ground, and have a studied 'raffinement' in contrast with the earthiness of Studio pottery.

England, in turn, produced her own group of Studio potters working in various techniques ranging, as we shall see, from salt-glazed stoneware, through high-fired, glazed earthenware, to the finest lustre glazes. One particular family of potters, the Martin Brothers, are interesting in that their work shows a distinct evolution from works of pure Victorian grotesque Gothic to works of Oriental-inspired simplicity in keeping with the Art Nouveau mood. Robert, Charles, Walter, and Edwin Martin, looking, with their eccentric, shaggy beards and ingenuous expressions, like four of the seven dwarfs from *Snow White*, were the first true British Studio potters when they founded in 1873 their workshop for the production of salt-glazed stoneware. This involved firing the stoneware at a temperature of 1450°C, and the light glaze was achieved by the potter throwing salt into the kiln at the correct moment. The roaring flames and critical timing made the process hazardous, and when one remembers that shrinkage at such temperatures could be one inch in ten, the risks become even further evident. The Martin Brothers' dedication survived various setbacks, and they won great praise for their grotesques during the 80s and 90s. As business was lagging towards 1900, they went to the Paris Exhibition of that year in search of new directions. The work of contemporary French potters, exhibited side by side with wares imported from Japan, had a profound effect on the brothers, and from this encounter dates their production of simple vegetable-like vases, such as the buff glazed gourd vase illustrated. The vases from this phase, lasting from 1900 to around 1910–14 are characterised in an article in *The Studio* of 1908. Many have interesting surfaces imitating fish or snake scales, lizard or leopard skins, or with vegetable textures, or employing the Oriental Mishima technique of inlaying clays of different colours. Many are of miniature proportions, the vase illustrated being an exceptionally massive $17\frac{1}{4}$ inches in height.

The Martin Brothers displayed the prime characteristics required of Studio potters: single-minded dedication to the clay they worked. No British potter, however, showed greater single-mindedness or dedication than William Howson Taylor, creator of 'Ruskin' ware. This man, lauded by his contemporaries as the world's leading Studio potter, from his first international triumph at the 1904 St Louis Exhibition through the Paris Exhibition of 1925 till his retirement in 1934, is claimed to have toiled 'for 36 years without a holiday. Twelve hours a day he has worked, every day, every year.' (*Birmingham Gazette*, Friday, 21st December, 1934). Huge sums were offered for Mr Howson Taylor's glaze recipes, but he took his secrets to the grave, having no interest in capitalising on his experiments. A reputed £20,000 were offered by A. F. Wenger, director of another Midlands pottery and, incidentally, the former owner of the vase illustrated. The

'Ruskin' pottery vase. William Howson Taylor, 1906

Glazed earthenware vase.
Die Wiener Werkstätte,
about 1910

vase was made in 1906 and was purchased as a good example
of the high-fired or *flambé* glaze, the secret of which Wenger
so envied.

Ruskin ware *flambé* pieces were fired at a temperature of
1600°C, and only Howson Taylor fully appreciated the
chemical reduction processes involved in achieving the
delicious colours and textures which aroused the curiosity of
the Japanese themselves. We find delicate duck-egg blues,
moss green, lavenders, mouth-watering plum or rich *sang-de-
boeuf* glazes, speckled, streaked or finely pitted, generally

on moderately thick bodies but occasionally on bodies of eggshell thinness. Howson Taylor's skill was such that he was able to take up successfully a challenge to fire a vase that had no earthenware body, but was made only of glaze! The Ruskin potter was not deeply interested in form and was happy to use variations on traditional Oriental shapes. We find ginger jars, depressed or elongated mallet-form vases, and various unassuming shouldered baluster, teardrop or onion silhouettes. His glazes would triumph on any base, and, at last, are being seriously re-appraised and being granted the prestige they deserve.

Ruskin ware had been given a bad name by the large proportion of commercially-produced wares available. This includes various low-fired textured wares and lustre wares which are often very harsh in colour. The fashion for lustre glazes which Howson Taylor helped cater for dates back to the 1880s. The first incentive was given by the Frenchman, Clément Massier, who rediscovered the different skills which he admired in old Islamic and Italian ceramics. Before long, few countries in Europe were without their experimental lustre potters, and by about 1900 many had achieved great competence. Among the experimenters were William de Morgan in England, Illyse Cantagalli in Italy, Herman Kahler in Denmark, and Vilmos Zsolnay in Hungary. The latter was responsible for certain pieces in strong Art Nouveau style, modelled naturalistically in full relief, as flowers or even as maidens with serpentine hair, or with linear Art Nouveau motifs on more conventional shapes. Zsolnay's work is characterised by the repeated use of ink blue and wine red, shading to purple. In England the Pilkington works launched, in 1903, their 'Lancastrian' ware which achieved superbly controlled lustre decorations with an extensive palette ranging from blue/black and deep red to pale yellows and apple green. This lustreware was subsidised by the parent firm as a prestige product, and though, arguably, it surpasses other contemporary lustrewares in its consistently high quality, the choice of subject-matter was too much restricted to the folklore of Art and Crafts Medievalism.

If the English could, in their decorated wares, be easily side-tracked onto the path of romantic Arthurian legend, other countries made a more positive contribution to the sum of Art Nouveau ceramics. In Austria we find advanced designs emanating from the Wiener Werkstätte workshops. Michael Powolny and Dagoberte Peche, under the watchful eye of Josef Hoffmann, started in 1903 their production of almost proto-Art Deco style pottery. Their symbolic bacchic putti, their dishes and covers, or vases, were generally decorated in stark, formalised black patterns reserved on a white ground. The shapes often betrayed a tendency towards the geometric which anticipated the styles of the 20s.

Apart from such slick exceptions as the mirror-perfect glazes of slip-decorated Rookwood, American 'Art' pottery of the turn of the century generally displays an evening-class roughness. Whether it was a question of quite gifted amateurs doing their best, or of professionals cultivating a 'crafted' look, is open to argument between the critics and the admirers of this school of American pottery. The Van Briggle and Grueby studios produced pieces, often broadly modelled with stylised Art Nouveau leaf or plant patterns, in particularly esoteric matt glazes. These demanded more of an acquired taste that did the charming pots decorated in naïve, stained-glass window flower patterns, in the manner of Eugène Grasset, made by the women at the Newcomb College which was founded in 1895 to encourage female interest in the crafts. Louis Comfort Tiffany invested a good deal of money in experimentation and created some of the more interesting American glazes.

Finally, in Holland, we encounter what have been called the finest of all Art Nouveau ceramics – the stunningly fragile, wafer-thin porcelain made in the Rozenburg workshops in The Hague. The eye is invited to trace swollen curves as they sweep into delicate flat planes, or the flowing lines of square-section loop handles or spouts which are drawn so graciously from bulbous bodies. All over these surfaces swarm painted decorations, birds of Paradise, flowers from the garden of an aesthete, delineated in hairline wisps of mauve, lilac, green, yellow or ochre, in the seductive, irresistible palette of *fin-de-siècle* preciosity.

Eggshell porcelain vase. Rozenburg, about 1900

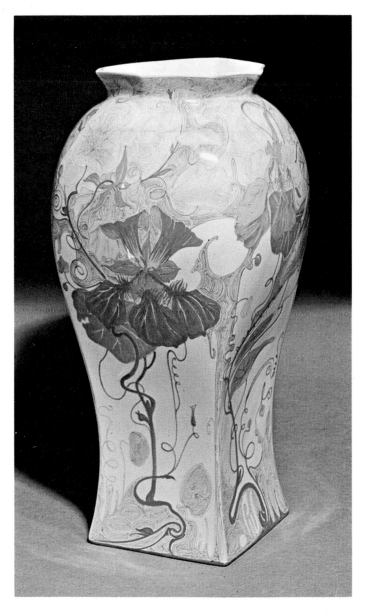

67

FOLIES-BERGÈRE

La Loïe Fuller

POSTERS AND PRINT

Lithography was the printing process favoured by the leading poster artists of the turn of the century. Indeed, if it had not been for the progress made in the development of this technique and the possibilities it allowed, the streets, first of Paris, then of cities throughout Europe and America, could never have been enlivened as they were by countless large, decorative, and colourful advertising posters. So popular were these posters that they inspired a generation of collectors who apparently thought nothing of stooping to crime to secure particularly coveted prints. There are many stories of bribes to printers or bill posters, parcels purloined from post offices and surreptitious midnight forays to peel posters from hoardings. When advertising commissions were not forthcoming, artists produced a slightly more sophisticated offspring of the poster, the *'panneau décoratif'* (decorative panel).

Lithography was invented as early as 1798, in Munich, by the Czech-born Aloys Senefelden. The process involved printing from stone blocks onto which the drawing has been transferred in grease pencil. Colour tones were built up through three or four successive printings from a set of blocks representing the primary colours and black. The thick stones could be rubbed down and subsequently re-used.

Daumier is perhaps the most notable of the many who experimented with lithography during the nineteenth century, before the advent of Jules Chéret, the artist who revolutionised poster art. With financial support from the perfumer, Rimmel, Chéret founded his own printing firm in the 1870s, introducing new machinery that, although still cumbersome, was capable of printing large-scale posters. The infinite subtlety of colour that could be achieved so inexpensively by lithography guaranteed the success of the poster as a popular art form. Armies of avid private collectors created a demand that shrewd printers were happy to satisfy, especially as, on large editions, costs could be cut down dramatically. It is sad that profiteering too often got the upper hand and publishers, eager to pare down costs to a minimum, used poor quality papers which survive

Lithographic poster by Jules Chéret, 1893

only in a brittle and yellowed state. Chéret, whose name always features prominently in any account of the Art Nouveau poster, was never truly a part of the movement. His celebrated poster of 1893 advertising Loïe Fuller at the Folies Bergère, is possibly his most 'Art Nouveau' work; but who could successfully portray Loïe Fuller in anything but high Art Nouveau style? Chéret's significance is as a technical rather than a stylistic innovator. His designs depict, with monotonous regularity, frothy laughing women, delicious and pretty, their tipsy features showing only the signs of never-ending carnival revelries, and the immediate comparisons are rather with an eighteenth-century *fête galante*, a scene by Watteau or Fragonard, than with the stricter stylisation of Mucha or Georges de Feure, even of Toulouse-Lautrec.

Lautrec is the second key figure in the story of the Art Nouveau poster. He profited earlier, and perhaps more directly and efficiently than any other, from the lesson that was to be learnt from Japanese art. During the early 1890s, Lautrec drew his celebrated series of posters of Montmartre subjects, which included *Le Divan Japonais, Jane Avril,* and the *Moulin Rouge.* These display in their collage-like structure, and in their use of bold silhouettes and strong outlines, a gutsy and un-diluted appreciation of the implications of Japanese two-dimensional art.

While, in Lautrec's work, we see the Japanese wood block as a primary interest and influence, in the work of truly Art Nouveau designers we see the Japanese influence absorbed indirectly, subtly blended with other influences, each playing secondary rôles to the more important cult of the Art Nouveau line. The most talented of these designers was Alphonse Mucha, and so concentrated was his expression of the 'Style 1900', that at the peak of his success 'Style Mucha' became one of several popular expressions to describe the new style, especially where the reference was to ethereal flower-bedecked women with formalised macaroni hair. Alphonse Mucha was born in 1860 in a small town in Southern Moravia. He was brought up in a most unpretentious household and in the tradition of the Roman Catholic Church. His background plays a crucial part in his art. Immediately recognisable in his work is a certain mid-European ecclesiastical opulence with

The Carnation.
Lithograph by
Alphonse
Mucha, 1897

relics of the Byzantine and heavy traces of a Roman Catholic Baroque. Some of his decorative figures are clad in costumes derived, surely, from heavily embroidered capes, and many of his *panneaux décoratifs* take on the quality of secular icons. Mucha betrays his origins in his simple fondness for a buxom and wistful peasant beauty. His women have a healthy romanticism that prevents even his most elaborate designs from becoming over-sophisticated or precious. More important, however, than this, in an understanding of Mucha's motivations as an artist, was his passionate pride in being a Slav, and his despair at the dissemination of his race. We must remember that Mucha felt his artistic duty lay in depicting the history of the Slav people, and this he did in a series of giant canvasses towards the end of his life when the fashion for Art Nouveau was past and fewer demands were made on his time. The decorative work executed during the 90s and early 1900s which has made Mucha's name so celebrated was not, in his eyes, his greatest achievement. Perhaps it is because the scope of Mucha's artistic vision and his spiritual sincerity were so much greater than this decorative style which for a while contained him, that his work has a depth of feeling that makes it more than mere decoration.

The story has been told many times of how Mucha's high Art Nouveau style crystallised after his first catalystic encounter with Sarah Bernhardt. Mucha was in the right place, at the right time, when on December 26th, 1894, a poster was urgently ordered for the opening of Mlle Bernhardt's new play *Gismonda*. Mucha sketched out an idea, apparently on a café table-top, which met with no sympathy from the anxious printer but which, fortunately, enraptured the actress, who, on the strength of this design, retained Mucha as her poster designer on a six year contract. The period of their relationship saw the flowering of Mucha's style and the production of his best-loved lithographs. His celebrated posters for Job cigarette papers date from this period, depicting women with demented scrolling hair, and with an air of mysticism achieved by one dares not guess what mixtures of grasses in their cigarettes. So also do his sublimely languid and romantic series, *The Four*

Panneau Décoratif. Lithograph by Alphonse Mucha, 1897

Lithographic poster by
Manuel Orazi, 1900

Seasons (1896) and *The Four Flowers* (1897). Mucha's enormous popularity led to a stream of commissions for every conceivable form of print design, from posters and panels to invitations, calendars, menu cards and book illustrations. One of his more unusual commissions was for the postage stamps and bank notes for the newly-formed state of Czechoslovakia in 1918. The abundance of Mucha's two-dimensional work makes it too easy to forget that he also proved himself a highly competent sculptor, as we have seen, jewellery designer, as we shall see, and designer of furniture, interiors, stage sets, enamels, ceramics and costumes.

In popularity, Mucha was second to none, which makes it hard to comprehend how Robert Schmutzler, the historian of Art Nouveau, could have compiled a book on the style without mentioning him. Several other artists working in France were gifted as designers of lithographs, and must be acknowledged. Georges de Feure, the Amsterdam-born artist, was as versatile as Mucha, creating furniture, fabrics, wallpapers, glassware and ceramics, in addition to a highly sophisticated series of posters, illustrations and decorative panels. In these we find the same imaginary landscapes that we saw as silk panels in his furniture, peopled with elegant greyhounds and intriguing women in exotic orchid gardens, and clearly the product of a highly refined sensibility.

Eugène Grasset produced posters and panels very different in character from those of de Feure. Instead of the latter's fine taut lines describing areas of muted pastel or autumnal tones, we find a strong, formalised stained-glass-window-like patterning and a heavy Medievalism. The reputation of Manuel Orazi rests on two posters of particular merit designed at the time of the Paris Exhibition of 1900. Orazi, a painter of Middle East-inspired exotic scenes, exhibited at the Salon des Artistes Français, and designed jewels for Meier-Graefe's shop, La Maison Moderne. In 1900 he directed his talent towards capturing the spirit of Art Nouveau dance in a poster for the Théatre de Loïe Fuller and in another for the Palais de la Danse. These two ephemeral structures occupied neighbouring sites at the Exhibition and the posters which advertise them have several features in common. Both are of tall, vertical proportions, both fade down into areas of swirling abstraction and are littered with Japanese-inspired motifs, among which we find included the artist's stylised monogram. The Art Nouveau style was created by a group of gifted designers, but then became a kind of patron in itself. Orazi is an artist who clearly profitted from the inspiration he found as the result of his encounter with the style.

Whether the Belgian posterist Privat-Livemont was a *pasticheur* or a true creator, is a subject of dispute, and has been since he was first dismissed by several contemporary critics as being merely an imitator of Alphonse Mucha. Privat-Livemont was Belgium's leading poster artist, enjoying his greatest successes during the second half of the 90s. His style leans heavily on that of Mucha, with its use of light or dark outlines to highlight and emphasise contours, its formal asymmetry and love of meticulously drawn detail work. His colours are more individual, however; they are more intense than those of Mucha, and, as a result, possibly more effective for the hoardings; his arabesques are more restrained and, however derivative, his work has the merit of being immediately recognisable. So, for better or for worse, does the work of the Dutch artist, Jan Toorop. In the celebrated poster which he designed in 1895 to promote Delftsche Slaolie, a salad oil, we seem at first glance to be confronted with a graphic maze puzzle in which the viewer is invited to enter the box and to find an exit through the confusion of parallel lines. In this poster Toorop uses a brand of Kitsch symbolism which is very open to mockery. The fetish for flowing tresses, which can be traced back to Rossetti, is here exploited as a trick to fill space, to alleviate Toorop's evident *horreur du vide*. The Dutch artist does, in all fairness, deserve more than facetious dismissal. He evolved his version of the Art Nouveau style with individuality and his drawing *The Three Brides* is considered an important contribution to the development of Art Nouveau. No lesser artist than Charles Rennie Mackintosh owes a certain debt to Toorop's graphic experimentations.

The British poster should perhaps have been discussed first, as it stands up poorly when viewed in the shadow of the great French posterists. Seldom can British turn-of-the-century

Lithographic poster by Jan Toorop, 1895

S. LANKHOUT & Cⁱ

poster art be truly described as Art Nouveau, displaying, as it does, the brash vigour of the Edwardian character, rather than serving as a vehicle for aesthetes. Aubrey Beardsley's importance as a crusader in British two-dimensional art cannot be under-estimated, and he succeeded in teaching a generation of posterists the value of certain techniques of visual short-hand, learnt to a great extent from Japan. Dudley Hardy, best known for his *Gaiety Girl* and *Today* posters has been raised by his admirers to the level of a British Chéret, sharing as he did the Frenchman's interest in representing flirtatious females. The comparison is unwise, however, for where Chéret achieves the airiness of Chantilly cream, Hardy, immutably British, offers us clotted cream. Hardy's virtue lies in his boldness in cutting up his large surfaces into blocks of strong colour, and in his confident draughtsmanship. We find a similar boldness and confidence in the posters of the Beggar-staff Brothers, though their treatment of a subject is always more subtle, less colourful and less showy than that of Hardy. Their style is one of broad wood-block-like silhouetting in muted tones of grey, charcoal or brown, with sparing use of colour.

From 1894, when Chéret posters were introduced into America to advertise a New York theatrical production, American graphic artists became extremely sensitive to developments in Europe, and various art journals thrived on broadcasting the very latest trends, so that, by 1896, poster mania was estimated to have inspired the staggering total of over 6,000 collectors. The best home-grown draughtsman to be carried to success on the crest of this wave was Will Bradley, whose early encounters with examples of Beardsley's work opened the way for his mature style. Bradley produced many illustrations and posters in the Beardsley manner – though without Beardsley's unsavoury aftertaste – in addition to colourful posters, such as that illustrated, which shows the European style interpreted with individuality and vivacity.

The Chap Book Thanksgiving Number. Will Bradley, 1894

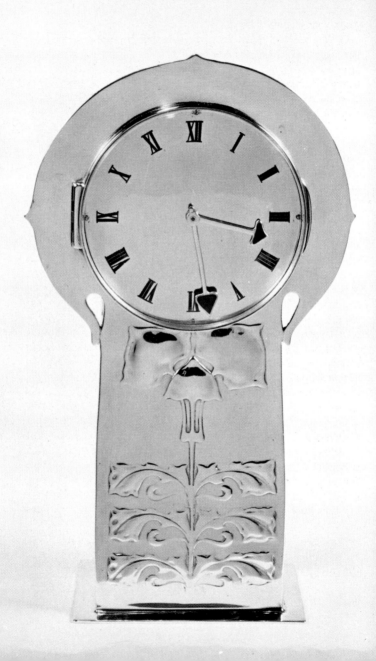

SILVER

For anyone brought up with typical examples of Victorian
silverware, overwrought, fussy and elaborate, and mixing
every type of mechanically or chemically textured surface, it
would be difficult to consider the metal in terms of the fluidity,
the sophisticated plastic quality of Art Nouveau. There was,
nonetheless, around 1900, a strong shift in attitude towards
the use of silver, and many craftsmen produced pure and
seductive examples of the Art Nouveau style in this metal.
The English were particularly successful in finding techniques
of exploiting silver in the new style.

Of prime importance was the new eagerness to bare the
metal. Dr Christopher Dresser was ahead of his time when he
designed his first totally plain silverware around 1880. His
work was so advanced in concept, with its geometric func-
tionalist purity, that it has more in common with the silver of
Art Deco designers like Jean Puiforcat, than with the Art
Nouveau silver for which it helped clear a path.

We find turn-of-the-century silversmiths freely using undecorated areas of mirror-smooth metal, the liquid quality
emphasised, perhaps, by fluid *entrelacs* borderwork of mer-
curic smoothness. Others exploited the intrinsic sensuousness
of silver by hand-hammering surfaces to achieve a softness, a
tactile appeal. This hand-hammering, as a sign of personal
craft in contrast to mass-production, underlined an ideal dear
to the English.

Good English Art Nouveau silver toyed with surface and
with texture; it also played with colour and we find many
examples of silverware incorporating areas of enamel or stone
cabochons to offset smooth areas of undecorated metal, or to
throw linear designs into relief. Alexander Fisher was amongst
the first to revive the use of enamels, and he decorated caskets
or other items with allegorical scenes in multi-coloured enamels. The most favoured colours for this generation of enamelists
were bright greens and blues, and a rich flame red. The cold,
strong blues and sharp greens were especially appropriate for
the cool sophistication of English Art Nouveau; not surpris-

'Cymric' silver and enamel clock. Liberty & Co., 1900

'Cymric' silver vase. Liberty & Co., 1902

(*opposite*) Silver and enamel jewel casket designed by
Archibald Knox. Liberty & Co., 1902

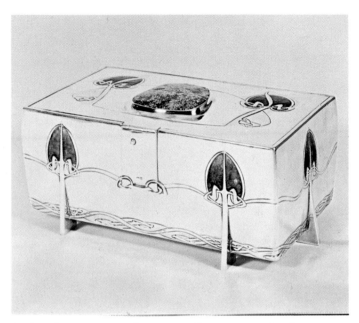

ingly, the most popular stones for use as cabochons were turquoise matrix, chrysoprase or Connemara. Certain designers added further contrast with a restrained use of mother-of-pearl. Neither the silver produced in other European countries, nor that made in America, could rival the consistency of English silver in providing the colourful and the unusual.

Two English schools of silver design can be distinguished; if, that is, we accept Dr Dresser's work as being in a third school unto itself. There was the English Arts and Crafts group, which included Omar Ramsden and Alwyn Carr, A. E. Jones, Gilbert Marks, William Benson, and Charles Robert Ashbee, designing for the Guild of Handicraft Ltd. This last named designer could, in certain examples of his work, be classed in the second group, that of the English ornamentalists, whose work has a more obvious slickness, an almost Continental polish which balances it on the fence between decadent Art Nouveau, the 'decorative disease', and reassuring English folksiness. Liberty & Co., with their stylish 'Cymric' range led the field in this second school, and their finer pieces rank amongst the very best objects produced in England around the turn of the century.

Liberty launched the Cymric range in 1899. This attack on the fashionable luxury market proved a great success, necessitating new workshops and considerably expanded production. By 1901, Liberty was employing the old Birmingham manufacturing company of W. H. Haseler to supply a strong demand for every kind of decorative silverware, from buttons, buckles or brooches to important jewel caskets, bowls, or tea services. The old Celtic word 'Cymric' was chosen as a trade name in acknowledgement of the debt owed in Liberty's silver to the elaborate *entrelacs* of ancient Celtic illuminated manuscripts, such as the *Book of Kells*, or to the decoration of Norse, Manx or Celtic crosses. We find these *entrelacs* exploited with taut control, sharing space with strong Germanic whiplashes or formalised plant motifs. Was the favour shown to the honesty plant, a disguised nod of acceptance to the principle of truth to materials?

Liberty & Co., in their desire to promote an awareness of their own image, maintained a strict policy of anonymity with regard to their designers. Research and cross reference have revealed, however, that the silver designing team was notably youthful, and included Bernard Cuzner, Rex Silver, the Scottish illustrator Jessie King, and, the oldest in 1899 – at thirty-five – Archibald Knox, an Isle of Man designer, who produced over four hundred designs for the Regent Street firm.

After Knox, Charles Robert Ashbee was perhaps the second leading exponent of English Art Nouveau in silver. Strictly, though, to be true to Ashbee's own principles, we should not categorise him as an Art Nouveau designer, for he was strongly opposed to what he deemed the excesses of the style. Visits to the Continent, however, on the occasion of exhibitions, left their mark on his work, and his reputation today rests largely on those pieces in which his clever use of sweeping and looping wire decorations shows the influence of Continental Art Nouveau. In his study, *Endeavour towards the Teaching of John Ruskin and William Morris* (1901), Ashbee explained his wish, in forming his Guild of Handicraft, to recreate the working

Silver mounted jug. Charles Robert Ashbee, 1901

85

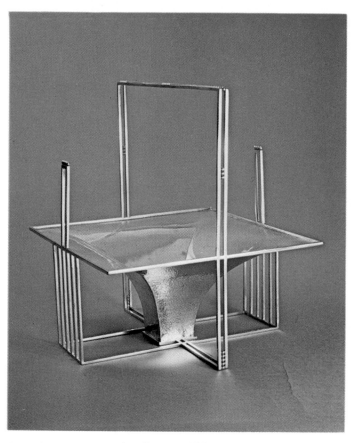

Silver fruit basket. Josef Hoffmann, 1904

conditions of a Medieval Guild. The Guild grew out of evening
classes at Toynbee Hall, and, all too often, these origins are
betrayed in a shoddiness of workmanship, which is the result
of inexperience and not of a deliberate effort to achieve a hand-
crafted look. It is when Ashbee's work escapes this blinkered
idealism of the Arts and Crafts movement that it achieves a
serene and mannered elegance of international importance.

Many from the English Arts and Crafts group could, to a
greater or lesser extent, be accused, together with Ashbee, of

being blinded by the romance of a mythical return to Medieval craft ideals. It is sad paradox that the laborious handwork demanded by this democratic ideal cost money, and so the enemies of the élitist system, the enemies of mass-production for a mute majority, became purveyors of luxury goods to the few who could afford them.

William Benson was a designer who succeeded in producing modest yet attractive hollow-ware. He is best known for his tea-kettles on stands, usually in silver-plated metals, which include themselves in the modern movement by their pursuit of an uncluttered and unself-conscious functionalism, rather than by extremes of styling. Omar Ramsden and Alwyn Carr registered their first mark in 1898. They designed very distinctive pieces, harking back in both form and decoration to Tudor originals, and reflecting that strong British yearning for the romantic spiritual port of rest of the great Age of Craft. Ramsden and Carr incorporated thistles and roses in hand-hammered pieces, which almost invariably bear the delightful inscription: 'Omar Ramsden et Alwyn Carr me fecerunt' ('Omar Ramsden and Alwyn Carr made me'). Charles Rennie Mackintosh, whilst hardly earning the title of silversmith, was responsible for an attractive range of flatware, in the attenuated, 'modernist' shapes of which it is not too far-fetched to see the origins of post Second World War Scandinavian designs. Mackintosh was an important source of ideas for the Vienna Secessionists, the Austrian School of Art Nouveau dominated by the architect/designer Josef Hoffmann. In their search for a visual vernacular capable of conveying their radical ideas on 'modern' design, the Austrians drew from the elegant geometry of the Glasgow School's work. Mackintosh and his colleagues, however, produced no silver to match that designed by Hoffmann, who conceived vases and other objects that were ruthlessly modern with their rejection of romanticism, their emphasis on hard, cold lines. Certain of his vases are as aggressively twentieth-century as the Empire State Building, and do actually achieve a skyscraper effect, with their strict vertical planes broken up into regular openwork squares, like the endless acreagres of window panes.

Hoffmann's silver designs, whilst generally involving a spartan angularity, have a tactile attraction which prevents

the designs appearing hostile. The piece illustrated shows how an impersonal feel is avoided by hand-beating the surface. Hoffmann's interest in texture induced him to create a range of more whimsical objects, vases or dishes with formalised floral decoration, scooped facets and ribbon scrollwork, which were fully hand-beaten. Certain of Hoffmann's designs were mass-produced in base metals and his work was much copied, but the originals stand out in combining pioneering designs and quality of execution.

The Belgian designer, Henri Van de Velde, designed various jewels and pieces of silverware which epitomise the best aspects of his work and of the Belgian School of Art Nouveau. Henri Van de Velde, who was, between 1899 and 1917, architectural adviser to the Grand Duke of Weimar, was primarily an architect, but, like Mackintosh in Glasgow, or Guimard in Paris, he found it impossible to resist designing in every medium and on every scale. He even created Art Nouveau dresses for his wife to wear in their Art Nouveau home. In 1893, Van de Velde explained: 'All my designs owe their character to one source alone – reason, and obedience to the laws of reason in conception and in construction.' His style is plastic, abstract, and emphatically linear, displaying a fine sense of proportion. His line play is imaginative, yet aims at a logic of construction rather than at a superficial frivolous appeal. Van de Velde designed buckles and brooches, samovars, tea services, and a celebrated candelabrum in his own strong version of the Art Nouveau style. The Germans produced little good Art Nouveau silver, being more concerned with the mass-production of decorative wares in silvered base metals. Nor, surprisingly, did the French excel as Art Nouveau silversmiths. French *orfèvrerie*, at the turn of the century, tended to be very conservative with few designers investigating the new style. Cardeilhac made attractive silver mounts for the vases of Emile Gallé, and are best known for a semi-Art Nouveau *chocolatière* (chocolate pot) decorated with thistles and with tinted ivory handles. In Denmark, Georg Jensen launched, around 1900, a simple, modern style of silverware that survives today with little change.

French silver pot and cover. Aucoq, about 1900

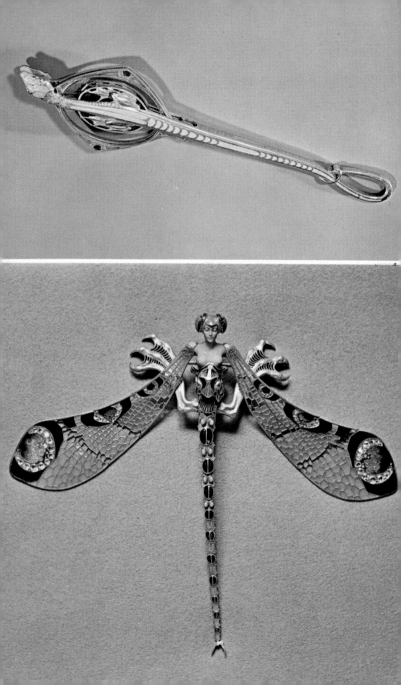

JEWELLERY

Daring was the woman who entered the lists at a *fin-de-siècle* ball, her chest adorned with a giant *parure de corsage* modelled as a fantastic dragonfly, or wearing a macabre metamorphic brooch, half woman, half butterfly, or holding a lorgnette, its stem a spiteful lizard.

For the extravagant, baroque jewels, created in high Art Nouveau style by artists such as René Lalique, Georges Fouquet, Henri Vever, Eugène Feuillâtre and others, were the jewels of the *avant-garde*. The woman who elected to wear such creations was, in doing so, declaring her sympathy with 'modern' ideals, and asserting her independence, her nonconformism. We have seen how the Art Nouveau style embodied a spirit of revolution. There exist Art Nouveau jewels which describe every manifestation of this revolutionary style, from the simple linear designs, produced by Liberty & Co. of London, in silver, enamels and semi-precious stones, the emphatic abstract creations of Van de Velde, and the geometric approach of Hoffmann and the Wiener Werkstätte, to the most important category: the exquisite, decadent creations of the top Paris jewellers. These must rank highest for the impeccable standard of their craftsmanship and for their originality and inventiveness. Not since the Renaissance had there been so successful a marriage between art and craft in jewellery.

Jewels have always been created to adorn women. French Art Nouveau jewels were created to adorn, but more especially to celebrate a particular breed of woman, 'La Femme 1900', whom we have encountered frozen in bronze, the sensual, pagan *femme fatale* of *fin-de-siècle* fantasy. A generation's dreams are found crystallised in the drugged creatures of Art Nouveau jewels. An orchid brooch, finely enamelled in speckled apricot and amber tones has at its centre a female face, perhaps a death mask, carved in moonstone. A jewel-bedecked young woman flirts playfully with the snakes that encircle her, whilst an ivory Medusa, surrounded by writhing serpents,

Lorgnette by René Lalique. Gold and enamels
Dragonfly *parure de corsage*. Gold enamels, chrysoprase, and brilliants. René Lalique, 1898

screams in torment, her staring eyes represented by opals. These typical themes show an idolatry tinged with perversity. Baudelaire called his decadent poems *'Les Fleurs du Mal'* ('The Flowers of Evil'). Here are *'les bijoux du mal'* ('the jewels of evil'), and frequently their self-indulgence leads them to cultivate the sinister and disturbing. Just as certain French glassmakers deliberately used insects or plants generally considered repulsive, so we witness French jewellers exploiting the grotesque and even elaborating on it in creations of pure fantasy. René Lalique's dragonfly *parure de corsage* is a nightmare image. This freak creature has no wings. From his body grow grotesque griffin's claws, and the delicate, translucent wings grow, in fact, from the shoulders of the chrysoprase woman whose naked body has been almost entirely devoured between the menacing dragonfly's gaping jaws.

For Lalique and his contemporaries, technical inventiveness was just as important as inventiveness in subject-matter, and under the auspices of this daring new generation of jewellers there developed certain new attitudes. The mystique of the precious stone, or the idea that a jewel should be merely a setting for commercially important stones was discarded. Art Nouveau designers were, on the contrary, more attracted by the opaque mysteries of semi-precious stones such as opals, moonstones or chrysoprase. In their search for the unusual they were attracted to misshapen stones. If, for example, a pearl were to be used, it would almost inevitably be a baroque or black pearl. Little importance was attached to the intrinsic value of the materials used. The value of these jewels is in the artistry with which materials were selected and juxtaposed, and, during the Art Nouveau years, we find an unparalleled range of materials employed, often of virtually no commercial value but treated as judiciously as if the rarest stones were in question. In 1893, the Belgian, Philippe Wolfers, used ivory imported from the Belgian Congo in his jewels, and in 1896, René Lalique exhibited jewellery incorporating carved horn. The eagerness of such designers to mix their materials eventually necessitated special legislation, and on 6th July, 1900, the Chambre Syndicale de la Bijouterie de Paris won its petition for an amendment to the law which forbade the use together of 'base' and 'precious' metals. The extensive use of highly

Brooch. Gold, enamel and moonstones. Eugène Feuillâtre, about 1900

sophisticated enamelling was another characteristic feature of
Art Nouveau jewels: cloisonné, champlevé, clear or opaque,
matted or lustrous, and, finest of all, wonderful *pliqué-à-jour*
enamels, played an essential rôle in their decoration. Often a
combination of enamelling techniques was used in a single
piece. *Pliqué-à-jour* enamelling was the most difficult, as it
involved firing the enamel within an open filigree work to
achieve an ultimate effect of sensitive translucence.

An article in *Art et Décoration* in 1898 drew attention to one
artist in particular who was working successfully in *pliqué-à-
jour* enamels. Eugène Feuillâtre worked in Paris as a jeweller
but his passion for this translucent enamelwork led him to
experiment on larger areas than those allowed by the limitations
of jewels. A dish in the Victoria and Albert Museum depicts a
frenzied flying fish in meticulous multi-coloured enamels in a
painstaking *tour-de-force* of *pliqué-à-jour* work almost twelve
inches in diameter.

Such elaborate craftsmanship was a luxury that depended
on patronage. René Lalique, for instance, owed a good deal to

Dish by Eugène Feuillâtre. Silver and *pliqué-à-jour* enamel, about 1905
(*opposite*) Bracelet by Georges Fouquet and Alphonse Mucha. Gold and enamels, about 1900

the sympathetic support offered him by Calouste Gulbenkian, who said of the jeweller: 'He ranks amongst the greatest figures in the history of art of all time, and his so personal masterly touch, his exquisite imagination, will excite the admiration of future élites . . .' Lalique, born in 1860, learnt his craft as an apprentice to the goldsmith Louis Aucoq in 1876; after a brief period of study at the Paris School of Decorative Art, and several years producing freelance designs for various firms including Aucoq, Cartier and Boucheron, he took over the direction of his own workshop, inherited from J. Destape in 1886. Lalique enjoyed the reflected glory of Sarah Bernhardt when the great actress, hearing of his talent, commissioned

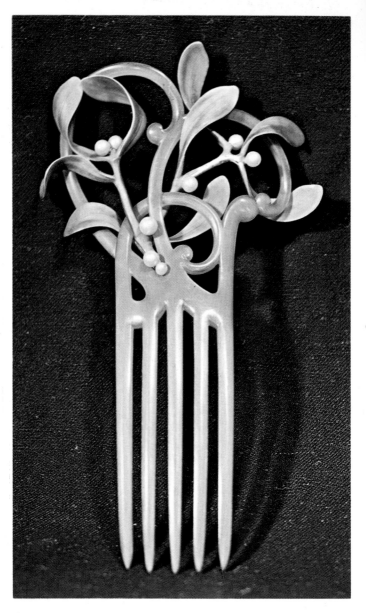

him to design jewels for her rôles in *Izeyl* and *Gismonda*, and general acclaim soon followed when he exhibited for the first time at the Paris Exhibition of 1895. He took away the third prize at this exhibition, though perhaps earned more attention in the year 1895 for being the first to incorporate a female nude in a jewel. Within two years his unparalleled talent earned him the *Légion d'Honneur*. Lalique was too curious and too gifted a craftsman to limit himself to jewels and his mixed media works of art, combining bronze or silver with ivory or cast glass, exude a refined preciosity. His interest in enamels and vitreous substances led Lalique to experiment in about 1898 with the all-glass creations that became an increasingly import-ant aspect of his work. Lalique eventually abandoned jewellery to devote himself during the inter-war years exclusively to the mass-production of good-quality well-designed glassware.

The name of Sarah Bernhardt, which featured at the outset of the careers of Lalique and of Mucha, features again, linked on this occasion with that of Mucha, in the story of the jeweller, Georges Fouquet. Born the son of a jeweller in 1862, Fouquet entered his father's workshop at the age of eighteen. When in 1895 he took over the management of the firm, he very soon up-dated its image allowing free play to his predilection for the Art Nouveau style. He distinguished himself at the Paris Exhibition of 1900, and after a long and illustrious career was named *Président des Bijoutiers* at the Paris Exhibition of 1925. The high point of Fouquet's career, however, was that brief period around 1900, when he worked in collaboration with Alphonse Mucha, transforming the latter's sketches into marvels of enamelled gold, carved ivory, semi-precious stones, and baroque pearls. The supreme legacy of their collaboration is the famous 'Serpent Bracelet' created for Sarah Bernhardt. Designed by Mucha for the first night of the actress's rôle as Cleopatra, this bizarre, finely enamelled and articulated ser-pent encircles the wrist, terminating over the hand in a grotes-que barbed head. Gold loops through his nostrils, and slender jewelled chains, link the bracelet to a matching ring. The story is told of Miss Bernhardt's difficulties in finding the money to pay for such an extravagance. Apparently Fouquet was obliged

Comb by Henri Vever. Horn and pearls, about 1900

to send messengers nightly to the theatre during the play's run in order to recuperate the money in instalments from the box-office takings. Mucha was inspired by Sarah Bernhardt to design at least two other jewels that were executed in Fouquet's workshops. One, in gold and enamel, contains a miniature by Mucha of the actress as Mélissinde in *La Princesse Lointaine*; the other, in various shades of gold and incorporating precious stones, depicts Miss Bernhardt in a relief portrait. Soon after 1900, Mucha completely redesigned Fouquet's shop in the Rue Royale. Opened in 1902, this was one of the most elaborate Art Nouveau interiors created, though it suffers from being over-wrought and oppressive. Two other Paris jewellers of merit were the Vever brothers, Henri and Paul, like Fouquet, second generation jewellers. Their standard was high, yet their work seems restrained, a little stiff in comparison with that of Lalique or of Fouquet.

Belgium produced one jeweller of outstanding merit whose work is closely comparable with that of the Paris jewellers discussed above. Philippe Wolfers was born in Brussels in 1858 into a distinguished family of goldsmiths. He was a gifted pupil at the Brussels Fine Art Academy and, after having been exposed at the impressionable age of fifteen to Japanese artefacts at the Vienna International Exhibition, was determined to use his talents to find an escape from the tyranny of the European tradition. Those pieces which he designed during the 1880s in his family workshops show strong traces of the Japanese and a return to nature for inspiration. The 1890s saw Philippe Wolfers establishing his own *atéliers* and winning acclaim for the unusual combinations of ivory and gold, which he first exhibited in 1893. It was to encourage trade and exploit the natural resources of the Congo colony that Leopold II made the gesture of offering ivory free for artists to create prestige pieces. Wolfers' talented exploitation of this opportunity marked the foundation of his reputation, and the delicacy of his interpretation of Art Nouveau motifs singled him out over the next few years for international praise.

If the precious creations of these jewellers discussed above are the produce of a rarefied hot-house, then the jewels produced contemporaneously in England can only be described as the produce of a fertile allotment. For the British tended to

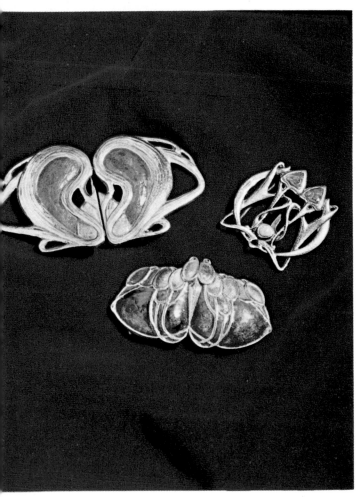

Liberty & Co. buckles. Silver and enamels

maintain rigorously their particular brand of aesthetic asceticism which precluded indulgence in the feminist whims and sophistications which were the natural inclination of the French. Oscar Wilde is describing his own fantasy when, in his *Salomé*, Herod offers 'Jewels that are marvellous. I have a

collar of pearls, set in four rows. They are like fifty moons caught in a golden net. On the ivory of her breast a queen has worn it . . .' Such imagery was too strong for the British, as it was essentially alien to their nature to equate jewels with emotive experiences. English jewellery was not entirely without interest, however, Two categories of jewels demand our attention within the British Art Nouveau movement. A small number of individual pieces were artist-designed in the Arts and Crafts tradition, whilst a second category promoted the ideals of the Art Nouveau movement by providing good clean designs at accessible prices. Within the first group we find a few intriguing jewels designed by the Glasgow Four, or the intricate work of Sybil Dunlop. Charles Robert Ashbee, better known as a silver designer, was responsible for attractive pieces such as the peacock pendant illustrated. Executed in gold and silver and set with diamonds, baroque pearls and an olivine, this jewel employs a symbol of which the Arts and Crafts movement was very fond. The peacock is restrained in contour and this, together with the deliberate 'hand-crafted' finish, gives the piece a distinctively English look.

It was as part of their effective effort to give an identity to British craft that *The Studio* magazine held competitions, encouraging amateurs to contribute designs. The designs for jewels and accessories, which were featured as a result, helped typecast that school of British design whose emphasis was on an abstract interpretation of natural forms. The most consistently attractive pieces in this vein were the buckles, buttons, pendants and brooches commissioned and retailed by Liberty & Co., their sensitive silver *entrelacs* thrown into relief by enamels, or incorporating cabochons of opal, turquoise, lapis lazuli or Connemara.

Pendant by Charles Robert Ashbee

'Tudric' pewter tea service. Liberty & Co., after 1903

METALWORK

No aspect of the applied arts was too humble for Art Nouveau designers to consider, and as much thought was given to objects destined to be made in pewter, cast iron, or other base metals, as to the enamelled gold or silver objects discussed above. In England, France, Germany or in the United States of America, certain designers applied themselves with pleasing results to metalwork design. England's outstanding contribution was the range of pewterware launched in 1907 by Liberty & Co. of Regent Street, under the trade name 'Tudric'. This project was the offspring of Liberty's successful silver range, a kinship emphasised by their similar Celtic names. Cymric silver had proved so popular that Arthur Lasenby Liberty became convinced that a more accessible range of domestic ware, in pewter, but designed along similar lines, would prove an even greater success. His hopes were fully justified, and certain of the designs were still in production in the 1920s, and exceptionally in the 30s. The sacrifice of all but four of the remaining moulds to the furnaces as a contribution to the war effort in 1939 marks the final curtain of Tudric pewter.

The Birmingham firm of W. H. Haseler was responsible for the manufacture of the bulk of Liberty's pewterware, though certain pieces bear the mark of Connell, 83 Cheapside. The quality of the moulding was good, *entrelacs* and stylised honesty motifs being executed with crispness and precision, though, inevitably, with repeated use, the moulds lost their definition, and later pieces can be distinguished by a loss of detail. Earlier pieces were also frequently enhanced with hand-hammering, and areas of blue/green enamel served to colour the pewter surface, which had a brightness as a result of the high silver content. Contemporary catalogues show a wide selection of items, including decorative tableware, vases, bowls, deskware, and tea and coffee services. A *Liberty Yuletide Gifts* brochure shows the complete five-piece tea and coffee service, perhaps the best known Tudric item, retailed at £5 8s. 0d. At such prices good design became accessible to a wide public and Liberty deserves credit for his successful compromise between art and industry.

In launching a range of artist-designed pewterware, Liberty

& Co. were reviving a metal that had been largely ignored for domestic use during the nineteenth century. If a strict chronology were observed, however, credit for this revival should be given to the German firm of J. P. Kayser Sohn of Krefeld, founded by Engelbert Kayser in 1885. Their production, sold under the trade name 'Kayserzinn', reached a peak around 1900, and their exhibit at the Paris Exhibition of 1900 came to the notice of the *Art Journal* which commented: 'In the gallery of the German section there were many exhibits of an artistic nature. There were few more worthy of our attention than the work in "pure tin" by the firm . . . It is a real pleasure to be able to record the high standard of excellence which was maintained throughout all the objects shown.' A. L. Liberty retailed Kayserzinn wares after 1900 and they appear in his catalogues before the introduction of his own Tudric ware. Kayserzinn was not the only German pewterware with which Liberty had tested his market, and his catalogues after 1900 also featured the productions of the Cologne firm, 'Orivit', and of the Nuremberg firm of Walter Scherf & Co. under the trade name 'Osiris'. He was the first to admit that '. . . alongside the foolish and undesirable, it must in justice be admitted that the Germans have recently produced many original and pleasing designs in pewter.' In addition to reviving the use of pewter, German manufacturers popularised the Art Nouveau style, or *Jugendstil* as they called it, by the industrial manufacture of silvered metalwares. Sadly, whilst bringing the style to a vast public, they were frequently guilty of debasing the essential ideas of the style, for they borrowed motifs haphazardly and can too often be accused of an insensitive commercialism. The largest manufacturing company, and the worst offender, was the Württembergische Metallwarenfabrik. Daniel Straub laid the foundations for what is, today, Germany's largest domestic metalware factory, with his workshop, founded in 1853 with a staff of sixteen, for the production of silver-plated copperware. The second half of the nineteenth century saw the mushrooming of the concern as it swallowed up smaller factories, and, by 1900, the W.M.F. mark could be seen on hundreds of

Silvered metal candlestick. Württembergische Metallwarenfabrik, about 1900

stamped-out objects catering in their facile ornamentation to a not-too-discriminating mass-market.

French metalwork designers, working in bronze or iron, managed, with a typically French flair, to maintain a feeling of luxury. Cast and wrought ironwork played only a small part in the French Art Nouveau movement, but assumed an increasingly important rôle in the years before the First World War in a transitional style between Art Nouveau and Art Deco, and after the war became closely associated with the Art Deco style in the elegant work of Edgar Brandt, Charles Piguet and Raymond Subes. Jean Dunand, the Swiss-born craftsman who became internationally famous during the 20s as a lacquer worker and *dinandier*, or worker in non-precious metals, after an apprenticeship to the mixed-media sculptor, Jean Dampt, made a series of Art Nouveau vases in textured and patinated metals, the irregular gourd or vegetable forms laboriously hammered from flat sheets of metal.

Louis Majorelle had a metal workshop at Nancy where, in addition to casting the ormolu mounts for his furniture, he cast elegant Art Nouveau bronze lamp bases, modelled as stylised plant stems and destined to support flower-form Daum glass shades. Majorelle's craftsmen made hammered iron mounts in late Art Nouveau style into which were blown Daum glass vases of a characteristic orange colour and flecked with foil. The Musée des Arts Décoratifs, Paris, preserves a fine example of Majorelle metalwork, a balustrade for a staircase in polished wrought iron, the oozing lines of the hand-rail surmounting elegant scrollwork and formalised honesty motifs. René Lalique chose the pine as a theme when designing the applied decorations for his new home in the Cours de la Reine which was the subject of an article in *Art et Décoration* in 1902. The author of the article admires Lalique's 'Japanese' restraint, his sense of balance and his logic, and draws our attention to the balcony design, where Lalique has applied his pine theme to the medium of wrought-iron with exquisite style and total mastery. The French master of Art Nouveau cast-iron was Hector Guimard. The architect designed cast-iron fittings of every description to adorn his buildings, and the freedom

Cast iron *jardinière*. Hector Guimard, 1907

Gilt-bronze and glass dragonfly lamp. Louis Comfort Tiffany, after 1900

allowed by poured iron encouraged his inventive and voluptuous linear style, always surprising the spectator with its unexpected asymmetrical complexities, or its bold sensuous abstractions.

The introduction of electricity for domestic lighting in the United States of America towards the late 1890s encouraged a fashion which soon swept the country. Within a few years no fashionable home was without its Tiffany, or Tiffany-style, lamp. Louis Comfort Tiffany's adoption of stained-glass techniques for use in electric light shades was perhaps his most significant contribution to functional commercial design, and the series of lamps which he marketed after about 1897 were his most successful commercial venture. The critic Mario Amaya admires these lamps as 'Tiffany's most satisfactory objects both from a plastic and utilitarian point of view.' The mushroom shades with their richly coloured and textured glass panes soften the harsh light of incandescent or, after 1903, of tungsten bulbs as well as concealing ugly fittings and, when not lit, provide a rich jewel-like series of colours and textures. In their fully sculptured, plastic conception, Tiffany's lamps exemplify the Art Nouveau principle of fully integrating form and decoration. When, for example, Tiffany designed the 'Wisteria' lamp (in collaboration with Mrs Curtis Freschel in 1904) he conceived it, not as a lamp applied with wisteria motifs, but as the tree itself, the bronze stem representing the trunk, spreading its roots over the circular base and supporting a deep, irregular shade incorporating glass panels, the colours of wisteria blossom and leaves.

The Wisteria was one of the most popular Tiffany lamps and was made in several variants of size and colour. A more elaborate variation on the same shape was the 'Lotus' lamp, the multicoloured shade representing hanging lotus flowers, their stems rising from the bronze base, clustered with overlapping lily pads. The lily theme was repeated in Tiffany's prize-winning 'Lily' cluster lamps, a design in which as many as twenty bronze stems rose up from lily cluster bases and supported individual gold lustre glass flower-form shades. The large gilt dragonfly lamp illustrated is a rich variant on a design by Clara Driscoll which won Tiffany a prize at the Paris Exhibition of 1900. Other designs chose flowers as their theme, the poppy, the tulip, the rambling rose, the daffodil, or the labernum. The bronze work of the Tiffany studios generally bears an embossed mark and the lamp-shades bear a metal plaque 'Tiffany Studios, New York', and a reference number on the inner rim.

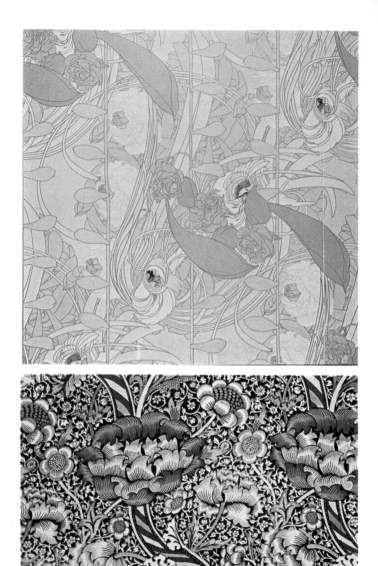

WALLPAPERS AND TEXTILES

Possibly the single most obvious sign of the re-awakening of general interest in Art Nouveau that occurred in England during the 1960s was the revival by large wallpaper manufacturers of the designs of William Morris and Charles Annesley Voysey. These papers are enjoying as great a popularity today and, indeed, have been as fashionable as when they first appeared. Their impact was first felt in the 1880s and they were made popular by Liberty & Co., with whose name they are still closely associated. Both Morris and Voysey based their designs on abstractions and stylisations from nature. Morris chose floral subjects which he formalised, usually by repeating a large motif, the repeats linked by scrolling stems, against a dense background of smaller flowers. His designs tend to be more naturalistic, and generally more oppressive than those of Voysey, who was responsible for cleaner abstractions from nature, generally rendered in lighter pastel tones. Morris's designs are usually proto-Art Nouveau, whilst Voysey's are more frequently pure examples of the style, his ideas more advanced. Both artists' designs were used for furnishing or clothing textiles as well as for wallpapers. *The Studio* magazine featured many interiors in which were incorporated papers and fabrics of the type associated with these artists. The effect is rather cottagey. English Art Nouveau designers would also decorate wall areas with stencilled friezes in naïve formalised patterns which would be repeated on pieces of painted furniture. M. H. Baillie Scott is the architect/designer most usually associated with this technique, though Charles Rennie Mackintosh was responsible for the most sophisticated stencilwork. He decorated walls in private houses with his elegant 'roseballs' and he decorated the Buchanan Street tearoom in Glasgow with human figure subjects entwined in elegant 'Celtic' strapwork. In Belgium, Henri Van de Velde covered walls with line patterns which repeated the structural motifs of the furniture within the room. His Havana Company Cigar Store is a good example of his ability to integrate every detail of an interior.

Textile design by Georges de Feure. Gouache, about 1900

Textile design by William Morris, 1884

PERSONALITIES

It seems almost incongruous to read Count Robert de Montesquiou reminiscing in his memoirs, *Les Pas Effacés*, published
in 1923, on the bewilderment with which he reacted to the
early manifestations of the Art Deco style. Montesquiou's
was a life of artifice and he was able to find a certain fascination
in the exotic fantasies of the Ballets Russes of Diaghilev. He
admired the décors of *Schéhérezade*, describing them, in out-
dated, precious style, as 'A combat between Cactus and
Amaranth, a carnage of Geraniums'. Yet he felt frankly old-
fashioned at the prospect of Cubist art or of the craze for
primitive African art. This hard, aggressive new taste seemed
so far removed from the mellow tastes of those years around
1900 when he had been a leader of fashion, 'Le Chef des Odeurs
Suaves', the distiller of sublime scents, a patron to the aspiring
and an inspiration to many. At the peak of the Art Nouveau
era, Count Robert had been one of an élite of aesthetes, a true
pacesetter for fashion and a catalyst for the creative.

The works of art discussed in this study are the tangible
relics of an era of art history. Yet it would be a sad omission to
consider them in isolation, to forget that they owe their entire
existence to the state of mind of those characters by whom or
for whom they were created. These objects are the reflection
of the modes and mores of their generation, and come to life if
considered in the context of the exotic characters, such as
Robert de Montesquiou, who were the flesh and blood embodiment of Art Nouveau. A close look at the lives of the personal-
ities who achieved prominence with the Art Nouveau movement reveals, in addition to their individual intrigues, a constant cross-weaving of events, a chain of reactions between
symbiotic characters.

The idea of people becoming works of art was a conceit dear
to Oscar Wilde and his 'aesthetic' friends. The Irish play-
wright must have been wild with delight as he observed the
extremes to which certain characters were prepared to push
themselves, extremes which included virtual acts of contortion-
ism, as desperate followers of fashion forced their bodies into

'Spy' caricature of Oscar Wilde

curves which echoed the arabesques of the 'Style 1900'. An extraordinary photograph survives of one rather delightful such attempt. Edith La Sylphe, her slender young form padded in parts and crushed in others, manages to exemplify the French axiom, 'il faut souffrir pour etre belle' ('one has to suffer in order to be beautiful'), without appearing ridiculous.

Her photograph shows a static attempt at twisting the female form into the Art Nouveau style. Today we can only imagine the impact of Loïe Fuller, the American dancer who captivated Paris with her act and whose movements were a magically intangible evocation of the Art Nouveau style. Bronzes or lithographs can only hint at her appeal. Marie Louise Fuller was born in a small town near Chicago in 1862. She was lured at an early age to the theatre and enjoyed moderately success-ful tours in the United States of America and in England. That she should become a dancer was the result of a succession of chance incidents. Loïe, for her stage name had, early on in her career, replaced her more pedestrian Christian names, had been sent a length of fine Indian silk by a young officer whom she had met at a dinner party in London. When the producer of a play in which she had a minor rôle decided that he wanted to portray the effects of, or at least create an illusion of, hypnotism, Loïe was asked to improvise. She wore the length of silk, flowing from her neckline, and, as she drifted in the dull green glow of the footlights, her audience was enraptured. Thus in 1891 she became, rather unexpectedly, the highlight of an otherwise un-noteworthy production. She had found her medium of expression and after months of practice with various lighting effects and elaborations on the flowing silks, and after years of hardships and disappointments, she found fame as a dancing embodiment of Art Nouveau. Ethereal, mystical, she danced as the Lily, as Fire or as Night, as a Butter-ly or a Bird. Isadora Duncan, in her autobiography, shows an understandable malice in describing Miss Fuller's private life, expressing mock naïveté at the spectacle of Miss Fuller's doting and exclusively female entourage; she succumbs to genuine appreciation, however, at the spectacle of Loïe Fuller on stage: 'That night we all sat in the box to see Loïe Fuller

Loïe Fuller cast in gilt-bronze. Raoul Larche, about 1900

Photographic portrait of Sarah Bernhardt

Loïe Fuller. Oil painting by Marie-Félix Hippolyte Lucas, about 1898

dance . . . Before our very eyes she turned to many-coloured, shining orchids, to a wavering, flowering sea-flower, and at length to a spiral-like Lily, all the magic of Merlin, the sorcery of light, colour, flowing form . . . I was entranced . . . this was a sudden ebullition of nature which could never be repeated. She transformed herself into a thousand colourful images before the eyes of her audience. Unbelievable. Not to be repeated or described.'

When Loïe Fuller was still an unknown, she had greatly admired Sarah Bernhardt, and when La Divine Sarah took a box, during Miss Fuller's second season at the Folies Bergère, so that she might pay homage to this new genius of Dance, the standing ovation accorded by the actress must have been a moment of deep pride. In a photograph taken in Miss Bernhardt's apartment around 1900, one can see on a mantel a bronze figure of Loïe Fuller dancing. It is a cast of the sculpture by Raoul Larche, which, most appropriately in relation to her dance, serves as a lamp, with bulbs concealed beneath the flickering folds of her drapes.

Loïe Fuller's artistry and vitality were concentrated on her stage performance. Her fans were frequently disappointed on meeting the rather plump and plain off-stage reality. Sarah Bernhardt, however, had a presence which commanded the same attention off stage as on stage. In her life, she acted out fantasies and became the embodiment of Symbolist ideas. There is a photograph of her asleep in a coffin which serves as a morbid reminder of this side of her character. Her taste in interior decoration, which could on occasion be appallingly bad, served a prime object of glorifying, almost deifying her person. She is frequently represented in splendid isolation sitting, aloof, under a large canopy, atop heaps of Middle Eastern cushions and animal skins.

Miss Bernhardt was a moderately talented painter and sculptress. A bronze inkwell by the actress, only recently re-discovered, is a self portrait in which she presents herself as a sinister harpie. Miss Bernhardt was demanding, extravagant and indulgent and, despite her own occasional lapses of taste, hers was a Midas touch and her personality inspired many outstanding works of art, such as the jewels by Fouquet or the graphic designs by Mucha discussed earlier. She won the admiration and the hearts of many, including even Oscar Wilde, who saw her as his *Salomé*, and the delicate Count Robert de Montesquiou, with whom she shared a brief but, inevitably, fruitless passion as early as 1876, and with whom she was to enjoy a sympathetic friendship for many years.

Robert de Montesquiou, an aristocrat, the descendant of d'Artagnan, was the great dandy of the *fin-de-siècle*, and, although he laboured over a series of volumes of Symbolist poems, it is not for these he is remembered, but for the image he left to posterity in the series of portraits of himself which he commissioned from various fashionable painters, including Whistler, Philip de Laszlo, Helleu and, above all, Boldini. Montesquiou was Art Nouveau itself, with a superficial frivolity, an urbane elegance which belied a background of intelligence and sincerity. The man, like the style, pursued absolutes of Beauty; in craving novelty he often achieved eccentricity but his humour saved him from ridicule. Montesquiou was not amused to be represented by Huysmans as the sickly decadent des Esseintes, the central figure in his novel,

Count Robert de Montesquiou, oil painting by Giovanni Boldini, 1897

A Rebours (Against Nature), and the model for Wilde's *Dorian Gray.*

He saw his as a dignified and active rôle and, undoubtedly, his encouragement was a valuable asset to certain designers. In particular, one can trace a strong link between Count Robert and Emile Gallé. They exchanged a vast correspondence,

and there exist several vases by Gallé with inscriptions taken from the Symbolist poems of Montesquiou. The Count is known to have commissioned various works from Gallé whom he describes as one of the conquests made by his first volume of poems *Les Chauves Souris (The Bats)*. Montesquiou sent a small group of selected friends copies of this anthology at the beginning of 1892 and these precious gift copies are works of art themselves. These special china-paper volumes came wrapped in silk on which had been printed a design of bats, and had delicate silk fly-leaves printed in *fin-de-siècle* grey on mauve with further bat motifs.

In his first volume of criticism, *Les Roseaux Pensants* (1897), Montesquiou championed the cause of Art Nouveau and, in particular, the work of Gallé and Tiffany. He is known to have commissioned from René Lalique a diadem of fuchsias as a gift for Mme Greffuhle and a peacock feather ring for Lady de Grey. He was even inspired to compose verses on Loïe Fuller whose dancing captivated him briefly. Montesquiou promoted Japanese art passionately, for a while, but his butterfly mind eventually found refuge in a return to the styles of the French eighteenth century. The vermicelli extremes of Art Nouveau were too absurd for his delicate sensibilities. Montesquiou was very much a society figure whose vanity and ideology demanded constant contact with the élite of society.

In Brussels there lived a character as bizarre as Count Robert and whose life was as much a product of the *fin-de-siècle* years, but who thrived on isolation. Fernand Khnopff was, like Montesquiou, an aristocrat who around 1880 first attracted attention for his very distinctive style of painting. He developed a manner which drew on Pre-Raphaelite art and on Japanese art – two great sources of Art Nouveau. More intriguing to the public, however, than the fact that his graphic work displayed elements of the new-developing Art Nouveau style, was the strange intensity of his subject-matter which succeeded in capturing the full depth of sadness of decadent *fin-de-siècle* symbolism. There pervades his work

Sarah Bernhardt in 'La Princesse Lointaine' by Marius Vallet. Gilt-bronze, about 1895

Sire Halewyn. Dry-point by Fernand Khnopff

that quality of sombre and sinister mystery which makes Art Nouveau so repellent to the uninitiated. His muse, and his almost exclusive subject-matter was 'La Femme 1900'.

Khnopff worked obsessively on the theme of an idealised symbolic female beauty. Her features are sombre, her jaw heavy; hers is a never-smiling face with cold, penetrating eyes. She would appear in his drawings or paintings in various guises, her head joined with the body of an eagle or a leopard, in opulent Medieval dress, or in plain contemporary dress, but with bizarre elements of stage-dressing: a solitary flower, a domino mask, a laurel wreath, a sword, or a winged death mask of her own features. The atmosphere was one of stillness, of lifelessness, of artifice and isolation. Khnopff drew from no model save his imagination, tasting cerebral pleasures in a beauty he never hoped to find in this world, and the character of his work was for this artist a whole life style. He lived in hermit-like seclusion in a serenely barren series of rooms, largely decorated in white and with only the odd single flower or precious object for decoration, and for company the effigy of his lamented tortoise, cast in bronze by René Lalique.

GLOSSARY

Agate ware, glass with the look of polished agate

Cabochon, a polished stone in an unfaceted dome shape

Cameo glass, layered glass cut away to reveal the underlayers

Cased glass, another term for layered glass

Clair de lune glass, glass with an opalescent sapphire tint

Clutha glass, a trade name used by James Couper & Sons for glassware designed by Dr Christopher Dresser. 'Clutha' is an old Scottish word for cloudy

Connemara, a green tinted marble

Coupe, a wide drinking vessel on a stem

Dry-point, an engraving technique

Entrelacs, intertwining decorative motifs

Favrile, Tiffany's trademark meaning 'made by hand'

Feathered glass, glass with coloured striations resembling feathers

Femme 1900, female symbol of Art Nouveau

Femme fleur, female symbol of the Art Nouveau marriage with Nature

Fin-de-siècle, 'end of century', implying the mood of decadence around the year 1900

Flambé glaze, term used by W. Howson Taylor to describe his glazes fired at high temperatures in the kiln

Glass trailing, glass applied in thin bands

Giltwood, wood applied with gold leaf

Jugendstil, Gérman term for Art Nouveau: literally 'youth style'

Lustre glass, glass by Tiffany, Loetz and others, with an iridescent surface

Marqueterie-de-verre, a technique used by Emile Gallé of inlaying glass

Millefiori, ornamental glass in which multi-coloured canes of glass are set within an outer layer; literally 'a thousand flowers'

Orfèvrerei, work in precious metals

Panneau décoratif, decorative panel

Parure de corsage, large jewel worn on the chest

Pâte-de-verre, glass paste fired and solidified at a high temperature

Pliqué-à-jour, translucent enamel

Salt-glazed pottery, pottery fired without glaze, but with a hard coating achieved by throwing salt into the kiln

Sang-de-boeuf, a deep oxblood red glaze

Secession, Viennese Art Nouveau movement

Sellette, a stand

Studio potters, the experimental potters working at the turn of the century

Style 1900, another French term for Art Nouveau

Verre double, glass with two layers of colour

Vide-poche, decorative dish or small piece of furniture, literally for the contents of one's pockets

Wheel-carving, method of cutting back cameo glass with a mechanically operated wheel

BOOKS TO READ

The French Poster by Jane Abdy. Studio Vista, London, 1969.
Tiffany Glass by Mario Amaya. Studio Vista, London, 1968.
The World of Art Nouveau by Martin Battersby. Arlington Books, London, 1968.
Art Nouveau by Martin Battersby. Hamlyn, London, 1970.
Art Nouveau by Martin Battersby. Studio Vista, London, 1971.
Carved and Decorated European Art Glass by Ray and Lee Grover. C. E. Tuttle, Vermont, 1970.
Posters by Bevis Hillier. Nicolson & Weïdenfeld, London, 1969.
Robert de Montesquiou by Philippe Jullian. Secker & Warburg, London, 1967.
Charles Rennie Mackintosh by Robert Macleod. Country Life, London, 1968.

ACKNOWLEDGEMENTS

Photographs
Agence Top, Paris, 93; Depot 15, Paris, 34; Mary Evans Picture Library, London, 112; Fratelli Fabbri Editore, Milan, 14, 96; Marc Garanger, Paris, 94; Calouste Gulbenkian Foundation Museum, Lisbon, 90 bottom; Hamlyn Group – Hawkley Studio Associates Limited, title page, 4, 11, 12, 13, 16, 19, 21, 28, 29, 31, 32, 33, 40, 48, 56, 60, 63, 64, 67, 68, 71, 72, 74, 85, 86, 88, 95, 99, 102, 107, 110 top, 116, 120, 122, 123; – John Webb 9; Hamlyn Group Picture Library, 24, 83, 90 top, 110 bottom, 117, 119; Phoebus Publishing Company Picture Library, 25, 27, 78; Philippe Garner, 22, 37, 38, 114; Sotheby's Belgravia, 8, 43, 44, 46, 47, 50, 58, 59, 77, 80, 82, 104, 108; Victoria and Albert Museum, London, 100; William Morris Gallery, Walthamstowe, 6.

The following photographs are reproduced by permission of:
Musée des Arts Decoratifs, Paris, 90 top; Musée National d'Art Moderne, Paris, 119; Museum für Kunst und Gewerbe, Hamburg, 14; Tate Gallery, London, 9; University of Glasgow, Mackintosh Collection, 24, 25; Victoria and Albert Museum, London, 67, 86, 95, 100, 110 bottom; William Morris Gallery, Walthamstowe, 6.

Other photographs have been made by courtesy of:
Jane Abdy; Ian Bennett; Editions Graphiques, London; Philippe Garner; Haslam and Whiteway, London; Liberty and Company Ltd.; Gawain McKinley; Martins Forrest Antiques; Michel Perinet; John Scott.